DISAPPEARING DADS

DISAPPEARING DADS

Dwight E. DeRamus Jr.

Trey Nickel Publishing

Copyright © 2017 Dwight E. DeRamus/Trey Nickel Publishing.

All rights reserved. No part of this publication may be reproduced, stored in a retrieval system or transmitted, in any form, or by any means, electronic, mechanical, recorded, photocopied, or otherwise, without the prior permission of the copyright owner, except by a reviewer who may quote brief passages in a review.

All Scriptures are taken from the New King James Version (NKJV): Scripture taken from the New King James Version®. Copyright© 1982 by Thomas Nelson, Inc. Used by permission. All rights reserved.

Published by Trey Nickel Publishing

Photo by Good Life Media Productions

Cover design by Cierra Cole Consulting
Cover image by Pexels.com
Interior design by Adept Content Solutions

Manufactured in the United States.

ISBN 978-0-9989023-4-0

Contents

Dedication — vii
Acknowledgments — ix
Disclaimer — xi
Introduction — xiii
Family Affair — 1
Lost Boys — 13
Girls Gone Wild — 27
Media Influence — 41
Impact the Community — 51
Do Ye Church? — 61
Final Remarks — 73
References — 85
About the Author — 93

This book is dedicated to my parents Lawrence "Larry" and Shirley Dooley. Mom, thank you for everything. There are too many to mention. Larry, thank you for being a wonderful example of what an authentic Christian man should be.

To my Dad, the late Dwight E. DeRamus Sr. Thanks for laying the foundation during the first six years of my life. Some of my features, likeness, and characteristics come from you. Thank you. I love you all so much.

Acknowledgments

First of all, I would like to give honor to my Lord and Savior Jesus Christ for allowing me to write this book. I believe and know that He is the author and finisher of my fate. He continues to give me grace and mercy so I will be able to complete this endeavor. This book has been placed on my heart for some time now. It was time to unravel the thoughts in my head and place them into print.

Second, I want to acknowledge my wife, Monese, and my sons, David and Daniel, for standing by me and supporting my dreams of becoming an author of nonfiction. Thank you for being a wonderful mother for our children and the wife I need in my life. Sons, thank you for being the best blessings any father can have. We have come a mighty long way, and I am looking forward to continue with our journey together.

Last but not least, I want to acknowledge my immediate family—Floyd, Rashaunda, Lenore, Susan and John, Tyra and Marc, Helen, Theresa, Erika, Senoritis and Taylor, and Joshua and Alexis. God bless each of you. I love you all.

Disclaimer

The author makes no representation that the subject of the book represents the entire body of this book. The publisher or the author is not responsible **to any person reading or following the information in this book.** Neither the publisher nor the author shall be liable to any party for any errors and omissions. Even if the errors and omissions lead to physical, psychological, emotional, financial or commercial damages, including, but not limited to, special, incidental, consequential or other damages. **References are provided for informational purposes only and do not constitute endorsement of any websites or other sources. Readers should be aware that the websites listed in this book may change.** Our views and rights are the same: you are responsible for your own choices, actions, and results.

Introduction

How often does one come across an individual who can share family life experiences of having both parents, then a step-dad, and then a divorce that lead to single parenting within the first eighteen years of his life? Well, this actually happened to me. During the first eighteen years of my life, I lived through three different types of family experiences. These experiences, along with the state of this world, erosion of families, passiveness of churches, influence from the media, misdirection of our youth, and plight of our communities have prompted me to write this book.

What do I mean by the title *Disappearing Dads*? It is the attack of the family structure. *Disappearing Dads* is a book written for all of us, especially the men. God not only created man first, but in all of His infinite wisdom He created everything and said it was good, but man was alone, and it was not good. Scripture reminds us that woman came out of man and man through a woman (I Corinthians 11:8). God's original plan for the family unit was to have a husband and wife, both present and taking roles to raise a child. Once the father is taken out of the equation, a destructive family cycle is set in which children will take all of that baggage into their marriages or relationships and reproduce it, passing it on to the next generation. This destructive cycle has been widely accepted by many as a normal family structure.

Each chapter in this book will break down important factors where man deviated from God's divine plan for family. Remember in the book of Genesis where not only God caused Adam to fall into a deep sleep, but created a helpmeet for him to whom Adam gave the name *woman*. It is Satan who initiated the division between mankind and God, but it was mankind who chose to be separated from God in the first place. It was Satan's plan then and now to destroy anything and everything that God has created, starting with the family. Can you see the consequences of sin with its impact on families since that fateful day in the Garden of Eden? Do you notice the similarities of behavior between children without fathers and children without the heavenly Father?

Scripture reminds us in Malachi 4:6, *"And he will turn the hearts of the fathers to the children, and the hearts of the children to their fathers, lest I come and strike the earth with a curse."* Father's hearts had to be turned to their children because they were obviously not aimed toward their children in the first place. God wants our families to be in harmony; however, when the family breaks down, the nation will be cursed due to lack of father leadership in the home.

When fathers are not in their rightful place as the head, mothers have to assume that role. Once the changing of the head shifts from father to mother, the children's stability is not balanced and God's order of family structure has been altered. Scripture says God is not an author of confusion (I Corinthians 14:33). Fathers must return their rightful place and restore relationships by turning their hearts back to their children, and the children will turn their hearts back to their fathers. We also must turn our hearts back to the heavenly Father.

There is neither such thing as a perfect man or perfect woman nor any perfect mate. If looking for a soul mate, one should be willing to accept some flaws in the individual just as Jesus accept your flaws. Too many of us are willing to accept Jesus Christ as Savior, but not willing to abandon the practice of sin. How can one say he or she loves God, but continue to be willing to stay in sin?

Going back to the Garden of Eden after Adam and Eve ate the forbidden fruit, God only called out to Adam. God holds the father responsible for the family. Other than scriptures, how else are young men to receive proper instruction to be good husbands and fathers? What kind of seed is planted when children are young, and what kind of harvest is reaped once they reached adulthood if the father is not there to help nurture and cultivate? Many of these answers are unfolding right before our eyes. They can be answered as soon as you open your front door or turn on an electronic device. Many of these children will most likely exhibit violent behaviors, engaging in sexual activity and abuse alcohol and drugs.

In the eyes of a child, the father is the first teacher. The Bible says in Proverbs 22:6, *"Train up a child in the way he should go, and when he is old he will not depart from it."* The involvement of fathers in the lives of both his sons and daughters is critical for the emotional development and sexual identity of each. Children are looking for love, guidance, and a role model in order for them to understand their defined roles. Only a father can teach his son how to become a man, exhibit for his daughter how she should be treated by a man, and how to stand in the gap between his family and God.

We should understand crime does not discriminate no matter how affluent or poor the neighborhood, but consider the reason why gangs seem to be prevalent everywhere. An absent father in the home can be heavily attributed to the ills in a given community. Take a sneak peek at churches in our given communities. The number of men in the congregation determines the strength and stability of the neighborhood. How many men attend church on a regular basis?

How do we set out to find the missing father? It is difficult for some of us to believe in a heavenly Father when an earthly father is not present or active in our lives. We must understand we often act like orphans because we do not know who our Father is. An unquenchable appetite is created when seek to fill that void left from our fathers. Jesus reminds us *"that those who drink of the water He gives we will never thirst"* (John 4:14). There is a glaring difference between what a father has given and what the heavenly Father wants to give.

Consequences from absent fathers create a host of problems. First, we seek approval of others. Often these others really do not care. Matthew 6:33 says, *"Seek ye first the kingdom of God and His righteousness and all these things shall be added."* Is God not enough? Second, we are seeking worldly pleasures (sex, drugs, gambling, or wealth). These always take away something and it never give back anything. Solomon in the Bible tried this, but it did not work. Nothing substitutes for God. Last, we are seeking to be affiliated with a group because we need a sense of belonging (gangs, cults, and other extreme groups). We need to first seek the His kingdom and submit to His will.

The Bible gives us a blueprint as to how we should live our lives. Man takes that blueprint and deviates from the original plan. Whatever God has created, man has deviated. Men must accept the call from God with the responsibility of being a prophet, priest, provider, and protector of the home. However, when given the call, too many men place their phone lines on call forwarding or disconnect the service altogether.

There is no guarantee two-parent households are more stable or loving or are able to prevent bad outcomes for their children. However, this is the divine order God has created for fathers and mothers as husband and wife and circumstances are worse when He is not the foundation of the family. Any child can fall victim to drugs, alcoholism, prison, or unemployment whether there is a one- or two-parent household. If a choice was made to have both parents or not, then both parents would be the much better choice. Therefore, I will always side with the Word of God. All of us have scars from the presence or absence of our fathers, but the question remains: how many open sores do each of us allow healing through the Word of God, or do we continue to pass it on to the next generation?

The consequence of fatherless homes has sin as its root. This statement requires repeating. The biggest issue with sin is that it feels good, it feels right, and it is fun while committing it. Apostle Paul made it abundantly clear about not wanting to sin, but doing it anyway (Romans 7:19). Teaching by the father seems to be vital for turning the hearts of the fathers to the children. God tells fathers over and over to teach their children. Men must restore their relationship with the heavenly Father *first* and then return to their rightful place in the home; once that happens, then the hearts of the fathers are turned back toward their children and the hearts of children are turned back toward their fathers.

Family Affair

Family is the institution that is under the greatest attack in our society today. Nothing has done more to destroy both boys and girls than the devaluation of fatherhood in the family unit. This darkness has created several types of family units: single-parent homes, grandparents, unmarried heterosexual couples, homosexual couples, and adoptive and foster parenting. Satan's attack on the family has existed since Adam and Eve and continued through today. There are signs of it all around us.

With the ever increasing rates of divorce, the acceptance of common-law relationships and the legalization of same gender marriages, we can see how successful Satan has been in twisting and perverting what God wants from us. Let us not get confused on this; just because society changes its definition of family does not mean it is right in the eyes of God. God's allowance is not the same as God's approval.

What is the definition of family according to scripture? Jesus responded to this question by responding in the

Bible to the Pharisees about divorce from Matthew 19:4–6 which states:

> Have you not read that He who made them at the beginning 'made them male and female, and said, 'For this reason a man shall leave his father and mother and be joined to his wife, and the two shall become one flesh'? So then, they are no longer two but one flesh. Therefore what God has joined together, let not man separate."

This is more than physically leaving the family nest. Goals, ideas, desire, and vision of each couple should complement each other through the Word of God. It should not take a village or governmental interventions to raise a family; this is not what God has intended. It was God who established the family. According to scriptures without a man and a woman initially coming together in marriage, there is no family.

We can look at family systems and see the breakdown of the traditional family. More and more families display the disappearing dad. The significance of his disappearance is either emotional or physical abandonment, or both, which causes psychological devastation on the children of both sexes. Part of this psychological devastation is children living in an unbalanced and unstable home. There is no teaching from the father. Mother is working one or two jobs to make ends meet. What kind of role models children are supposed to follow if dad is not present and mom is working long hours? Daycare and schools have more of an influence on the lives of children than parents.

As stated earlier, consequence of fatherlessness has sin as its root. There are examples of systemic destruction of the family. First, marriage is being redefined by society where there is common law or same-sex, and second, distinctions in gender roles have been diluted, thus eliminating the idea that men and women make unique contributions to the home. Single-parent families headed by women are the most common type of family today. Women are able to work and provide for families; therefore, we assume that if a child is somewhat financially secure, this eliminates the necessity of the father. Last, there is a movement to remove the father completely out of the picture altogether. Whether it is artificial insemination from an anonymous donor or the court system, the image of dad seems to be irrelevant. Again this is not what God has intended. The truth is one person cannot become two, but two people can become one.

A dysfunctional family is anything that distorts God's natural order and His purpose through concept and action that has sin as its root. All of us have some level of dysfunction in our families because we are imperfect by nature. Every one of our families has been struck by the difficulty of selfishness, idolatry, and pride. All family members participate in withholding secrets, avoiding other family members, unable to communicate, difficulty managing anger, or spreading lies about family members. The differences in the level of dysfunction come in when we adopt most or all these issues as normal part of our lives.

Dysfunctional families can be traced back to the beginning of creation. Adam blamed Eve for something they were both responsible for and got "evicted" from their home. Lot offered his daughters for sex to an angry horny mob of men outside of his home. Isaac and Rebekah played favoritism with their twin sons, which caused a twenty-year rift between the boys. Abraham lied to Pharaoh about his wife, Sarah, being his sister who caused a plague to Pharaoh's household. Finally, David did a poor job in disciplining his children. One son raped his half-sister, which caused the other son to murder him. Then the murderous son tried to hunt down and kill daddy David. Remember Satan plays an integral part of tearing down families since his job is to steal, kill and destroy (John 10:10). For these reasons, dysfunctional families are nothing new.

Looking for that so-called soul mate or someone who will complete us is a problem. No mate should be selected by "love at first sight" or beauty alone. Being single does not mean he or she needs to get married because many of these people are not marriageable material. What makes this a problem is when we want another human to complete us. Spiritually speaking, this is a form of idolatry. This will always create an issue. We are to find our fulfillment and purpose in God; however, at times we have the tendency not listen to His voice, or choose to do our own thing. Without God as the foundation, the relationship will not last.

God the Father is the Lord of marriage; each man and woman is charged with roles and responsibilities. Marriage is like a puzzle. Just as a puzzle is incomplete if there are pieces missing, so is a man incomplete without his wife and vice versa. God designed it so that the man needs the woman, and the woman needs the man. *"Nevertheless, neither is man independent of woman, nor woman independent of man, in the Lord. For as woman came from man, even so man also comes through woman; but all things are from God"* (1 Cor. 11:11–12). Both are equal persons and yet have distinct roles to fulfill in the family unit. The concept of family creates two essential elements: marriage and parenthood. God's love for us as His bride is like the love the husband must have for his wife. God's love, patience, and correction for us as His children are the same as the way parents should raise their children.

Living together before marriage is commonly accepted these days. Cohabitation is a convenience but not a commitment. This definitely reflects the concept of instant gratification in our society. Many people will not only commit sexual sins through cohabitation but will also build sexual intimacy based on lust and not love. The enemy wants us to pursue our own selfish pleasures. Some call it a trial run to see if a potential spouse is a suitable or compatible marriage partner. So many people do not see cohabitation as sin, nor do they care to make decisions that are pleasing to God that would benefit them in the long run. We tend to make excuses out there to justify our actions, believing we are right in our own eyes (Proverbs 21:2). Cohabitating contributes to the declining number of marriages and the increase number of children born out of wedlock. For these reasons people choosing cohabitation rather than marriage are creating dysfunctional family structures.

It's no surprise that the world rejects God's design of marriage. The number of people entering matrimony is far less now than years ago. Fatherlessness not only leads to the decline of marriage but also does not appear to be a viable option anymore. Marriage mirrors God's covenant relationship with His people. It represents the symbol of Christ and the church. Many people rush into marriage without considering God's perfect will. God takes the union of two people in marriage very seriously. He designed marriage to meet our need for companionship to give glory and honor to Him. Hebrews 13: 4 says, *"Marriage is honorable among all, and the bed undefiled; but fornicators and adulterers God will judge."* He does not want the covenant to be broken. Even though we are fractured and imperfect people, when it comes to marriage many of us are spiritually immature.

We get married for the wrong reasons, often bringing personal issues and problems from their past into the marriage. We marry to fix family issues or marry because of pregnancy. We marry because of the idea, not because of the person with whom we want to become one. We may also marry because it does not have anything to do with God. As a result, abuse, abandonment, adultery, and so much more happens in the marriage, which often leads to divorce unless both people seek God to help them heal and restore their relationships. Remember Satan takes pride in destroying marriages, especially those of people of faith. Families are systematically being dismantled and redefined; there are four ways or the four D's that can cripple a family unit.

First there is divorce. Marriages today have never been in more serious jeopardy. Whether you are a believer or not, the divorce rate is soaring; the number of adulterous affairs is skyrocketing. Women are more likely to initiate divorce than men. There are plenty of billboards and commercials advising divorce to the masses. Divorce is given as an option for self-interest and self-righteous hypocrisy. Chances are, when parents divorce, the mother would have custody of the children and fathers have to fight for visitation rights and joint custody. Divorce adds to the increasing numbers of fatherless homes.

When filing for divorce, we are quitting, breaking our marriage vows before God. There is severe damage that is done to families than that which comes from divorce. If a marriage relationship is not meeting my needs, then I can choose to leave. If the origin of marriage is individual choice and not what God has joined together, then what is the foundation of the marriage in the first place? 1 Corinthians 3:11 tells us, *"For no other foundation can anyone lay than that which is laid, which is Jesus Christ."*

Children growing up in dysfunction homes have a tendency to create their own broken families. Children of divorced parents are three times more likely to divorce when they get married, thus repeating this vicious cycle and creating more fatherless families. It still does not change God's plan for marriage. Scripture says God hates divorce (Malachi 2:16). God hates divorce because He intended for man and woman to be joined as one until they part ways by death.

Second, the death of a parent can have devastating and lifelong effects on the surviving spouse and children. Since this book is about fatherless families, we are focusing on the death of the father. Circumstances surrounding a death of a father creates varying degrees of instability for the rest of the family, especially because the loss is so traumatic. Examples of these circumstances can be anywhere from natural causes, murder, terminal illness, sudden illness, or accidents. The main thing about death is that it is unavoidable and beyond our control.

Identities on the part of the children can be an issue because there is no modeling from the father when death takes him away. Anger and depression are common coping mechanisms to help deal with the experience. It can take from years to a lifetime to recover, depending on the amount of support that was given. Death is one appointment all of us will make on time because of our sin nature we have inherited from Adam. Aging and death began on that fateful day in the Garden of Eden. Romans 5:12 says, *"Therefore, just as through one man sin entered the world, and death through sin, and thus death spread to all men, because all sinned."*

Next, there is detachment. This problem goes far beyond physical absence. Our families are starving for fathers, even if dad is around, but he may be detached emotionally. He is so far removed from his family that his presence has no impact on other family members. A detached parent is like a deaf parent who turns his back to the deep end of a pool in which his child is swimming, and he neither sees the child swim too far out nor hears his cries for help when he cannot get back to the shallow end. He has become consumed with work, hobbies alcohol and drugs or pornography. This scenario is commonplace in middle and upper class two-parent households.

There are times when, for whatever reason, fathers are incapable of supporting their families. Once they feel this way, many are detached and ready to leave the family. Scripture says if a man does not provide for his family he is worse than a nonbeliever (I Timothy 5:8). Many fathers today are so preoccupied with their own interests that they pay little attention to their family. Intimacy levels with wives are heading downward. Arguments ensue for no apparent reason. They have no idea who their children's friends are, what their interest are, or what habits they are forming in the social media arena. Scripture says to fathers over and over again to teach the children about the heavenly Father (Deuteronomy 11:19). We are getting a generation of children being raised on the world's values.

The fourth and final D is desertion. Fathers abandon their families for various reasons, ranging from depression, regret, finances, addiction or growing tired of responsibility. If a man is not connected emotionally, physically, and spiritually to his family, then he feels inadequate. This failure mindset leads to a downward spiral that usually leads to fathers checking out mentally and then physically. Once fathers feel he is less than a man, he will most likely leave his family. These are traits of selfishness because we have a desire to concentrate on our own needs and wants.

Since sin is the root of dysfunction, this is part of the consequence from the fall of Adam and Eve. Sin creates selfish interests, not a wonderful relationship with God, but a hunger for something that will never be quenched or fulfilled. Scriptures said to come and believe in Jesus and you will never thirst or hunger again (John 6:35). It's easy to see how children blame themselves for the abandonment; they often believe they are the reason for the family to split up. Abandonment by their fathers will have a lasting impact on children's future relationships.

Many parents are afraid of government involvement if they discipline their children; therefore they are relinquishing their parental authority. This, of course, contradicts the Word of God. According to Scripture parents must separate foolish sinful ways from the child (Proverbs 22:15). They are also responsible for the teaching and training of children (Proverbs 22:6). Disciplining children was meant to be done by mother and father in love with no bruises or cuts. Children are to obey and honor their parents in a respectful way that adds value to the family unit. Juvenile delinquency, drug and alcohol abuse, teenage pregnancy, welfare dependency, and child poverty are all consequences from a lack of discipline that can be directly traced back to fatherless homes.

The brokenness in families is all too common in our society today. The significance of the hurt and pain from these relationships have a profound effect on everyone from fathers and mothers to the children. Creation of unhappy marriages and unholy unions result when one of the parties focuses on selfish desires and fulfillment. The concept of family is supposed to create two essential elements: marriage and parenthood. Our families are in serious need of repair.

God has delegated responsibility in raising the children to both parents, and each has a role the other cannot perform. Parents can teach their children to respect their authority and expect their love and discipline. Young people can choose to wait until they have entered a marriage and built a family before they make a child. Grandparents can invest time and interest in their children's lives by being a support to the family, not a primary caregiver.

As stated earlier, people make time to do what they really want to do. The family must make time to be unplugged from all electronic devices and plug into God and each other. Time must be taken for reading and praying together and for eating and playing together. We can all agree that no family is perfect, but we can believe that God uses broken people from broken families to accomplish his perfect will and purposes (Romans 8:28). As families live out God's plan for them, God will be glorified, and families will be blessed.

In conclusion, the strength of families is the foundation of nations. God is the one who created the concept of family in the first place. Remember, the enemy's job is to steal, kill, and destroy families from outside or inside influences (John 10:10). In order to fight the battle against the enemy's clever attacks, we must recognize the pattern and let the Holy Spirit inhabit our lives. We must do our children a favor and establish a family as God defines it so they will grow up with a better understanding of God and the wonderful salvation he offers. We need godly leadership, respect, and love, along with fervent prayers and dependence on God. The marriage relationship must imitate Christ's relationship with the church. When that happens, people will marry first, have children, and guide their children towards the Father, a cycle that should continue.

Lost Boys

Marriage and fatherhood, at one time, were seen as being the highest aspirations in a man's life. Today, due to individualistic and self-centered goals, the highest aspirations of men seems to be monetary gain, career success, and personal leisure. Society is making a radical shift away from the importance of fatherhood, which is slowly eroding away from existence. The male identity is being suppressed and redefined. Systems are put in to place where circumstances remove fathers from the home and force mothers to raise children alone with or without governmental financial support.

Never before have so many boys growing up without knowing what it means to have a father. Boys without dads will have a more difficult time behaving and acting like men. This absence of a father is preparing them for lives of selfishness, immediate gratification, and extended adolescence, thus creating unhealthy and difficult relationships with women. This will immediately impact their roles as husbands and fathers. As a group they feel abandoned and were not given a blueprint modeling various roles of being a husband and a father. This also hinders protection, provision, and affirmation given from fathers to sons. Consequences of not having a father figure will have devastating lifelong effects.

It is becoming more difficult to find men who assume headship and service in the family circumstance. When God created man, one of the privileges given to him was fatherhood by imitating Him as Father through headship (Ephesians 5:1). The other privilege is service. These two working in conjunction with one another allows men to take on the responsibility of serving their family through godly, servanthood leadership as priest, prophet, provider, and protector of the family (Matthew 20:28). Men are ultimately charged with serving their families and leading them to Christ. Somehow these privileges that were bestowed upon men were wrenched away by society.

Identity crisis has reached critical mass proportions because boys who grow up without fathers are insecure and unaware of their identity. Confusion of identity roles occur when boys become men. This stems from frustration for fear of failure or anger for not been given a roadmap to husbandry and fatherhood. So many men are turning to escapes to numb the pain of not having his father in the home. Pain has a way of resurface when it is bottled up. Whenever there is an absent father, we will consciously and unconsciously fill that void with a substitute. Self-medicating through sex, drugs, alcohol, pornography, and work are selected choices to fill the void. These effects can manifest themselves throughout adulthood for boys.

Based on statistics, fatherlessness has severe consequences on family, schools, community, and society as a whole. Boys are at much higher risk of increased sexual activity, school truancy, dropping out, and criminal behavior. Boys who don't live with their biological fathers tend to act out their pain in violent and disruptive ways. Their behaviors can lead to noncompliance with authority figures: adults, teachers, and police while eventually landing them into correctional facilities or the graveyard.

The overwhelming majority of juvenile delinquents and adult prisoners are boys who grew up in female-headed households. In schools, they have behavioral issues and poor academic achievement, which lead to poor grades, suspensions, or expulsions. Since fathers are supposed to be protectors and providers, boys will most likely engage in violent illegal activities involving guns and drugs to provide some protection and generate income for the household short on money. Neighborhoods are quickly morphed into crime areas because of inadequate financial resources in homes, deficient funding for schools, no spiritual impact from local churches, and the lack monitoring of children.

Boys will imitate and emulate their fathers whether they are present or not. They need their fathers in order to properly transition into male adulthood. They will also look for their father's approval in everything they do, and copy those behaviors. The balance of affirmation and accountability given by fathers is critical for every son's development into manhood. If paternal attention, affection, affirmation, advice, and accountability were not available to boys during their childhood, then their lives will be a constant search for these things.

Without a father present, there is no wisdom passed on regarding work ethic, money and managing resources, sex and relationships, marriage and child rearing, and spirituality and religion. No matter what age the person is, there will be a need to fill in the void of his life always scratching the surface. Boys will live out what fathers leave in them. They will continue to pass on the generational curse of fatherlessness: not married, procreating children out of wedlock, and failure to fulfill role as a dad. Unless God intervenes, boys will not have the proper biblical knowledge and guidance needed to understand their responsibilities when they become fathers. For boys who want to be a good fathers and practice their role and responsibility as fathers, they must learn from a good role model who is visible, easy to imitate, and easy to learn from.

When fathers are absent from the home, mothers will try to replace the loss of a father figure. The replacement may be an adoptive father, step-father, or just a nurturing male figure in the child's life such as grandfathers, uncles, cousins, big brothers, coaches, or family friends who fulfill some of the father's responsibilities. She may also try to perform the duties of both mother and father by herself. For mothers who are working long hours and sometimes with more than one job, busyness on the job takes time away from the attention and direction needed in raising boys. Mothers are likely to be involved in relationships with boyfriends who will turn out not to be husband or father material. Boys involved in this scenario are much more likely to suffer physical, sexual, or verbal abuse because of the men their mothers bring home. Scripture reminds us about knowingly failure to do the right thing and its consequences (James 4:17).

We have way too much mother and very little father in raising children, especially boys. Their identity is being formed by mothers who are raising them. Mothers who are raising the boys to adults play a significant role. There is a tendency for some boys in fatherless homes to reject their masculinity and accept femininity since mothers are the only role models with fathers not present to affirm their identities.

Even though this is more of a correlation rather than causation, the root cause of homosexuality or any other sin for that matter, is the human heart because it is so desperately wicked (Jeremiah 17:9).

Another issue of over-mothering creates a mindset in boys that women must be the ones to take care of them. An atmosphere of dysfunctional relationships occurs when a man will become the child, and the woman becomes the mother. This creates dependent men looking for independent women with financial means to take care of them. When raising boys, mothers must walk that fine line between being too dominant, which turns sons into abusive control freaks, or being too dependent, which turns sons into weak, passive men.

We live in a time where divorce, infidelity, promiscuity, and cohabitation are considered normal. These behaviors cause a significant relationship issue between men and women. The beginning of any relationship seems to be great at first because each person is on their best behavior. As time passes, the true definition of character and the relationship will come to light. These relationships struggle when its foundation is flawed from the very beginning.

What typically happens in many noncommittal, sex-only relationships is men act interested in women and they move in to live together, but she becomes pregnant and left to raise the child alone. Women are objectified because they were strung along while being viewed as a convenience of comfort and avenue of sexual pleasure. She was presented with empty promises in her mind and selfish feelings planted in her heart. Everything was offered to her except a marriage covenant.

A rift in the family unit was created when cohabitation outweighs the importance of marriage. The Bible speaks clearly against cohabitation in I Thessalonians 4:3–5: *"For this is the will of God, your sanctification: that you should abstain from sexual immorality; that each of you should know how to possess his own vessel in sanctification and honor, not in passion of lust, like the Gentiles who do not know God."* In other words, we should abstain from sex outside of marriage. This is a general pattern of how men fail to marry these women and the children they produce without fathering them. Women are forced to lead households and raise children alone, which they not are specially designed to do.

Men have not realized their purpose and direction to be cultivators, teachers, and the head of their households. There is no excuse for men to act like morally illiterate boys instead of mature adults. Society measures a man by how hard he works, how well he protects his family, or how tough he is. Sadly, many men across this nation and the world are either caught up in the judicial system or living sexually promiscuous lifestyles while spreading their seeds around everywhere. The world also diminished the need of a man in a family because he is being systematically replaced from his position as the head.

Once relationships and marriages are severed, children are often in the middle of the war between their parents for custody rights. Generally speaking, mothers would get custody of the children, and fathers are left on the outside. More and more fathers are absent for various periods of time in the lives of their children. Noncustodial fathers of all races tend to have difficulty maintaining relationships with their children. They feel hurt and pain when they are apart from their children. Most fathers don't want to leave their children. Their absence is significant, but whether or not there is quality involvement is critical. They love their kids and want to be engaged in every aspect of their lives. On the other hand, there are fathers who are not with their children's mother that are involved with their children's lives. Any positive involvement with the father is much better than none at all.

There are men who unable to find jobs because the jobs available does not provide enough income to support a family. If they happen to have a police record then the job outlook is even worse. When a man impregnates without any commitment, a heap of trouble will follow him financially and emotionally. Satan has put systems in place where there is great difficulty for men to do what God called them: provider to their families. Once the ability for a man to provide for his family is removed from him, then his roles as protector and provider leave the home, and the rest of the family suffers. This is included in the plague of fatherlessness.

Men are genetically wired to provide for their family, but when there are no jobs available they begin to check out, abuse drugs and alcohol, sleep around, or engage in illegal activities to survive. Many men believe there is no sense of going out in the job market with fewer qualifications that beat the odds of making an honest living. On the other end of the spectrum, we have men with financial means conduct unlawful secretive activities in businesses to acquire more money. When a father believes he must hustle or find illegal means of income, he will wind up pushing his family away.

Some fathers believe they can buy into their children's lives. They try to give them everything they can, except the things that really matters most. Children need love, time, sacrifice, personal attention, and training instead of material possessions. Financial support is great, but daddy support is better. Making purchases when these responsibilities have not been met is completely absurd. What children treasure most is the relationship with their father. Money will substitute for time with children.

Manhood is in constant conflict as it is redefined by society as opposed to how God defines it. Society has created this distorted view of what manhood supposed to be. Boys grow up learning these views of masculinity because fathers are not there teaching and showing them. These are nothing more than myths of authentic manhood. Four common myths will be discussed to show how unrealistic and destructive they are because they lack the qualities needed for becoming a successful man, husband, and father.

First, there is a need for dominance over others using strength and physicality through competition. Value is placed on a man's ability to win at all costs. Second, men were taught as boys to suppress their emotions by avoiding crying because it is a sign of weakness. This suppression of emotions makes it difficult for men to express themselves other than using anger. Next, an accumulation of sexual conquests in the bedroom creates a distorted view of relationships based on appearance, physical physique, and sexual performance. This myth generates an environment of no intimacy or commitment, thus destroying healthy relationships as previously stated earlier in this chapter. Last, the amassing of large sums of money is a mistaken belief of manhood. Money is important but not more important than God. This creates an atmosphere of materialism, power, and control instead of a spiritual atmosphere.

By examining these myths of manhood, it is clear there is an unrealistic cycle of pressure for men to conform. Many will follow this broad societal definition of manhood, but if this cycle is not harnessed with the Word of God, it will lead to destruction (Matthew 7:13). We must remember that every man is a male, but every male is not a man.

When choosing a mate a real woman is not perfect, and a perfect woman is not real. It's no secret how men view the attractiveness of a woman's face and body when selecting potential partners. All of us are broken people in one way or another due to our imperfections. Knowing this we must ask ourselves how much of their imperfections are we willing to work with. The key is to look past the world's standards and look to her heart (I Samuel 16:7).

It is the man's job to make a woman he loves a wife before he makes her a mother. This is God's original design for a family. According to His standards a man must first learn how to be a husband. Understanding his role and responsibility of taking care of a wife should be done first before taking on responsibility to children. Husbands are to love their wives as Christ loves the church, modeling the love of the Father in their most important earthly relationship (Ephesians 5:25). When a man loves his woman based on performance, he will expect his wife to stay or become beautiful. When a man loves like Jesus, he will beautify his wife as time passes regardless of the body's natural decline. A husband must fulfill his responsibilities by letting the Holy Spirit guide him, and this cannot happen unless there is a relationship with God (I Corinthians 2:13).

Children are not only a responsibility for fathers but a privilege. They are precious gifts from God. Fathers must realize that responsibility does not end at conception. God not only created man to love and cherish his wife, but he must also validate and affirm his children. God sets the example of fatherhood after Jesus' baptism in Matthew 3:17 which states, "This is my beloved son whom I am well pleased." Love, affirmation, and validation were given in one verse.

An authentic father is one who seeks to obey and honor God, sets a good example for his family, and models what it is to be a child of God. He is also the one who is responsible for his children by being accessible, engaging, listening, and spending time with them. Fathers are expected not only to train up his children but also to provide discipline as well (Proverbs 22:6 and

3:12). This is done with love without provoking children to be discouraged or angry. Fathers are told over and over again to teach the children.

A call of responsibility to families from the Word of God was given to fathers' roles as priests, prophets, providers, and protectors in the home that must be modeled and passed on to their sons. They must exhibit the attitude of servant in order to fulfill these roles properly. The Word is the only exact and reliable source for instruction. Family transformation will occur once these roles are embraced and followed. These universal truths are applied to all men in all cultures all over the globe. This will combat what society falsely defines as their role and purpose in the family structure.

Fathers must be priests in the home. They represent their families before God. Fathers must be able to petition God in prayer on behalf of his family. Fathers are to pray for the welfare of their wives and salvation for their children. Not only do fathers set the spiritual temperature in the household, but they are mediators between God and their family. Praying out to God must be done with some boldness and not in a passive nature (I John 5:14). Fathers are ultimately responsible for being the spiritual leader in their home.

A prophet hears directions given from God (John 8:47). In order to hear these directions, there must be an established relationship with open lines of communication with Him. Fathers must be representatives of God before his family and be able to instruct their family through Scripture. Fathers must also lead their families to church. They will have a better understanding of who God is and the importance of fellowship. Fathers are ultimately responsible for leading his family to God.

A provider must be will to sacrifice own needs, and if fathers do not provide all these things for their family, God says that they are worse than an unbeliever (I Timothy 5:8). Why? Believers have some biblical knowledge principles on how to raise children, care for their family, and love their wife. Even nonbelievers make sure they do not to leave their family unattended and not supported. Fathers are ultimately responsible for ensuring that his family's financially, physically, and spiritually taken care of.

A protector is one who protects his family from any hurt, harm or danger (I Peter 3 7). The physical nature and strength of men is to be managed with self-control. Self-control also includes faithfulness and keeping commitments. Giving into infidelities, not paying a debt, or not keeping a promised word leads to emotional heartbreak in the family. Fathers are ultimately responsible not only physical protection but emotional, spiritual, and sexual protection as well.

In the human life cycle, the boy becomes the father. The son carries on the vision of the father just as Jesus carried out the vision of the Heavenly Father. Luke 2:49 tells how Jesus responded to Mary and Joseph when they were looking for him in Jerusalem. *"Why did you seek Me? Did you know not that I must be about My Father's business?"* Fathers must be active members in their homes, churches, and communities. Stop falling to bad decisions. It's time for men to step up to the plate.

In the human life cycle, the boy becomes the father. The son carries on the vision of the father just as Jesus carried out the vision of the Heavenly Father.

God must be the foundation for everything and first in priority. A father must be able to lead his family with servant attitude. They must fulfill their role in their homes, church and communities. The job you work, the car you drive, the house you live in, or the money in the bank account does not define who you are. Real men are men of integrity, internal strength in Christ, courageous, willing to do what is right and to stand for truth at all times and in all circumstances. Men must submit themselves fully to Christ, and He will delight himself in you (Psalm 37:4). God has called men to be priests, prophets, providers, and protectors of the family.

Girls Gone Wild

The effects of an absent father are most often reflected from the pain of the male child only. However, the pain can also have devastating effect on the female child. Girls draw conclusions about what men are like from the men in their lives, including fathers, present or not. These conclusions create a conscious template engraved in the minds of girls about what to expect of men and what to expect of men's attitudes and behaviors toward women. If fathers are not present in the lives of girls, then there will be a series of damaging consequences ranging from self-esteem, intimacy, trust, sex and other fatherless-figure issues throughout their lifetime. The pain hurts so much that not enough words can express the pain when the father is missing from the home.

Fathers are the girls' first interaction with the masculine gender. They are the first man who able to give attention, hugs, kisses, and, more importantly, unconditional love. The relationship between fathers and daughters prepares girls for their unique roles as girlfriends and wives. Many fathers have placed their daughters on a high pedestal among all other girls. They are able to provide skills that will help girls develop self-confidence, self-esteem, positive expression of what love feels like, and appreciation of face and body images. A father's ultimate responsibility is to build his daughter's trust in men and prepare her as a capable partner for a future husband.

The impact of fatherlessness in our society is staggering. Our girls suffer as much as boys but with more internalizing behaviors. Fatherlessness has severe consequences on family, schools, community, and society as a whole. Girls from fatherless homes are more likely to be poor, become involved in drug and alcohol abuse, drop out of school, and suffer from health and emotional problems. They are also most likely to become pregnant as teens and engage in delinquent behaviors or date boys who practice these antisocial behaviors.

Girls who grow up without fathers in the home are lacking the wisdom and insight fathers can provide. They desperately want their fathers to notice her, affirm her, and love her. Fathers can instill in their daughters the ways of men's behavior toward women. Fathers are examples of how women should be treated by the way they care for mothers (I Peter 3:7). However, if fathers are absent from their daughters' lives, then they will seek attention in other ways.

Efforts to damage the family and family life are being sponsored by advocacy groups and other societal movements. These groups create the mindset that marriage is overrated. Mothers are able to work and provide for their families on their own. If the children are financially secure from a large enough income, then this eliminates the financial necessity of the father. The distinctions in gender roles have been distorted. This eliminates the idea that men and women make unique contributions in the home. Many women believe it is not realistic to depend on men for income. Furthermore, they believe the idea of marriage is an option, not a necessity for a strong family unit.

Are women turning into the men they longed for as little girls? Identity issues are apparent when masculinity is imitated. Some are even becoming men through fashion and genetic alterations by dating and marrying women. This is a way of compensating, a void bringing their fathers back.

Women are outnumbering men in education and employment fields. The days of running household and managing children are being replaced with acquiring houses, cars, and other material possessions through career achievements.

Most girls have already had premarital sex by the time they finish high school. These behaviors are most likely to happen in fatherless homes. No matter how much mothers showered them with love and attention or made sure all of her needs are met, it is still not enough. Some are even foolish to believe they can do without him, but impact of his absence affecting future relationships with men clearly tell another story. The lifelong pain and emotional baggage is carried with them to from one relationship to the next. Girls are always trying to compensate for the attention they may not have received from their fathers in her relationships.

Girls will naturally be influenced by their mother on how to be a woman like her. Since many of these women did not have fathers in their lives, they fail to see their value in the lives of daughters. Girls have been taught to look for earning potential, security, and ambition when selecting a partner while character, integrity, and sacrifice take a back seat. They witness their mother shoulder the burden of raising children without the help of a man. There is a mindset in some circles building a case for single parenthood as evidence of the increasing independence of women. This is simply dead wrong.

Relationships with boys are usually toxic from the very beginning because the foundation was not rooted in biblical principles. Generally boys would say anything that girls needed to hear in order to get them to do what the boys wanted them to do. Girls would in turn provide sex in hopes of receiving the love and companionship not given to them from their fathers. Boys, on the other hand, receive the pleasurable enjoyment of the physical act. Fathers would teach girls that their self-worth is between their ears and not between their legs.

Fatherlessness affects his daughter's choice of a mate and behavior in relationships. The lack of fathers is what girls will permit, and the benefit of fathers is what girls will expect in their relationships. The level of fathers' involvement seems to be connected to signs of certain behavioral characteristics for girls as they approach adulthood. Some of these characteristics affect the type of man chosen, emotional boundaries, intimacy, and abandonment issues that obvious in these relationships.

The lack of father involvement can pull women in different directions when encountering men in relationships. Women generally stress physical and emotional protection they should have received from their fathers while growing up. Therefore, many of them choose to date a much older man—at least fifteen to twenty years older—and wind up marrying her "daddy." Women are attracted to these men because of emotional maturity and availability of financial resources they can provide. Oftentimes the value of these men serves a purpose for them as father figure rather than a life partner.

Not recognizing emotional boundaries creates another issue that is not healthy for women. This lack of a father affects women's assessment of their value dealing with men. Women can be prone to abuse or victimization because they are so love starved that they tolerate broken relationships. Either they accept the role as being the other woman or stand by abusive controlling men. They tend will get more than what was bargained for, not realizing what other packages come along with men.

Another type of behavioral issue is the lack of intimacy with men. It is a way of fulfilling needs by bringing back the father they were missing while growing up. This usually leads to a promiscuous lifestyle by giving up their bodies without any emotional connection. Sex is used as power to garner the attention by visual stimulation through provocative clothing and seductive behaviors. Some also use sex for financial gain through the adult sex industry. Sadly, many women believe their body is all they have to give.

Finally, the fear of abandonment creates unfulfilled counterproductive relationships because of not wanting to end up alone. Women tend to look for starting fights or finding flaws or testing men because they expect to be abandoned. In this situation they have a tendency to be extremely jealous, clingy, and overly protective. Unresolved issues reach the surface when circumstances trigger the possessive behaviors. When controlling tendencies are not managed properly, there is a sense of losing power that must be regained by controlling others. Lofty expectations are never met because men will never measure up to what women believe their fathers are supposed to be like.

Controlling behavior is the cornerstone of abuse whether it is physical, verbal, or mental. Women with children make a serious mistake when being involved with these types of men. The boyfriends or husbands chosen will most likely abuse your children rather than their own. They will also manipulate and abuse you to keep you under control. Love is not supposed to be painful or leave bruises (I Corinthians 13: 4–5).

Sex outside of marriage is sinful and dangerous, and it will bring troubles in life (I Corinthians 6:18). Cohabitation may seem to be a more suitable option than marriage, but it brings more trouble than it is worth because its foundation is based on selfishness. Men are receiving the benefits of a wife without the commitment and responsibility. Many women move in men hoping to change them and eventually being proposed to by them. Only God can change the heart of man if he is willing (Ezekiel 36:26). This creates pseudo-wives when there are children born out of this common living arrangement.

Women will date and engage in sexual activity with a series of uncommitted men. There are many red flags or stop signs visible in the beginning of relationships, but they continue to roll right past them. Generational curses occur where the grandmother was a single mom, the mom was a single mom, and now the daughter is a single mom. So many failed relationships can create situations where children are born from different fathers. Other poor choices are made where women end up in a situation where they are both pregnant and not married or in a broken relationship.

There too many mothers and not enough wives. They should be wives before being mothers. Women who grew up fatherless are usually the ones producing fatherless children, which perpetuates the dysfunctional cycle of fatherless homes, violence, and poverty. There must be a balance between mother and wife. Unfortunately, the pendulum is swung toward the mother side and will not return back to the balance between the two anytime soon.

There are slim pickings for eligible bachelors. Schools, courts, workplaces, and prisons play significant roles of the limited number of potential suitors. The pool is even scarcer if looking for a mate of color. However, this does not mean settling on having a man at any cost. Women deserve to be loved, treasured, and valued. A significant amount of time should be spent watching and observing a would-be partner through various situations.

Women would often say that they want a "real" man. This tired term is too vague and does not give a clear definition. Remember, when choosing a mate, a real man is not perfect and a perfect man is not real. However, if a woman says that she wants a strong spiritual man who takes his instructions from God, a life partner to take a spiritual journey and grow old with, and the ability to lead a family gives a clearer meaning. The question should be, what kind of woman are you? Ladies must find a man who is in the right relationship before God. Otherwise, he will not honor and treasure you, he will not make you feel loved and cared for, and he will not be willing to lay down his life for you (I John 3:16).

Mothers do an outstanding job in raising children, but they were not created to do this task alone. When they love their sons and raise their daughters, a final nail is hammered in the coffin for future meaningful relationships and marriages. Girls being raised strong and independent create a false sense of security because it affects their encounter with the male gender. Boys are misguided, empty vessels continuing to search for identity because no man spent enough time with them, showing the ways of true authentic manhood.

Society creates lies about true womanhood where there is confusion of its meaning. There are characteristics of false womanhood where women do not trust God and are always looking out for their own interests. These self-serving behaviors continue to be responsible for the destructive cycle of broken families. This is leading to the myths of womanhood. The myths of independence, self-centeredness, and self-perception will be discussed to show how unrealistic and destructive they are because they lack true qualities needed for becoming a successful woman, wife, and mother.

Developing independence from adolescence to adulthood is one thing, but being independent of a husband is sinful. This independence caused Eve to sin. It also creates a false invincibility of not needing a man to rear a family, yet in reality she is being heavily assisted by her "artificial" husband. Her "artificial" husband is either her career or government through financial means. She believes in having it all, including having children without the financial support of a husband. Too much time is spent on careers, children, and chasing after wealth where there is little room for marriage. She was never taught how to get and keep a man instead of his seed. Women were created for companionship not to be self-sufficient.

Some women believe they should be the center of the universe instead of the center of God's purpose. Many women take pride in being self-centered and for caring only about their own levels of fulfillment. Women tend to overcompensate through careers, education, and appearance to deem themselves worthy. They require a constant need for praise and approval. When priority in life is given to self, activities, or objects instead of God, then it becomes an idol. The Bible specifically warns us about idols in Exodus 20:3–5. This is the end result of never receiving validation from fathers while growing up during the childhood years.

A self-perception issue is an indicator where fatherless women were not reminded of their beauty, value, and worth. Our society seems to be fixated on ideas about body image shown in magazines, commercials, and other media outlets. It is a strong influence for women about how others define them. Unfortunately, women fall into the trap believing they will be better or more valuable if they look better. They are willing to pay for expensive procedures to alter their body, imitating the world's false view of beauty. God sees each of us as a masterpiece being wonderfully made by His works (Psalm 139:14).

Popular thinking will have us to believe that submission is wrong and for the weak. It is perceived as putting your foot on someone's neck or controlling someone with strings like a puppet. Submission in its correct form is a sign of strength, not a sign of weakness. Submission doesn't mean you go along when you're being asked to do something that violates the word of God. This boils down to one essential question: do you follow society or do you follow Christ?

According to Scripture one must be filled with the Spirit with submission done out of the love for and obedience to Christ (Ephesians 5:18 and 21). Submission is more than serving your husband. It's about serving the Lord. God commands wives to love their husbands and the children. They are to be self-controlled, which means to constantly strive to be sinless in their lives. God will bless wives who are submissive to their husbands when they do it out of reverence to Him.

An authentic woman knows how to be a partner and helpmeet, not the head of a marriage. This *helpmeet* term is not taken lightly for it has such a rich meaning because it centers upon the very character of God. Psalms 121 is a reminder of the help God can provide for all of us. The Bible says that God created the woman for the man (I Corinthians11:9). She understands she is different than man; she is the complement for the man, and she has different roles in marriage than the man. Women are much more than the ability of bringing life into the world. They have been blessed the capability, resources, and strength to be a help to the family through support, service, and sensibility (Proverbs 31).

A good, supportive, trusting wife is a blessing to the family for an authentic woman. She holds the keys in keeping God's vision for family life. The biblical ideal is for men to provide for their families and for women to stay at home to raise the children is contrary to what is really happening today. Society has the economy set up where women are forced to work outside of home to generate more income. They are the main instrument in driving men toward or away from the will of God.

Being of service to God, her husband, family, and neighbors is another wonderful trait for a real woman. Having faith to serve the Savior first will guide her toward His will. She makes sure others are served out of her willingness to work to ensure all needs of those under her care are met. Financial household resources are managed wisely through conferring with her husband. In order to resist foolish spending, she makes sure purchases are based on needs first rather than wants.

A real woman seeks to obey God and understands the importance of making sensible use of her time spent with Him. Her appearance is respectful, and her well-being is intact in the community as a representative of the family. Some of the benefits for following God are gaining wisdom on how to raise godly children in an ungodly world (Titus 2:4–5). Daughters would be taught what it means to be a virtuous woman, and sons would be taught what to look for in future wives. This must be balanced with love and the Word of God.

God doesn't want his daughters to be taken advantage of and treated as pseudo-wives. God wants His daughters to be treasured by a man who would lay down his life to serve and protect her. They should not be burdened with stress, lead the relationship, or come up with ways to pressure men into marrying them. Men were created for leadership, and they are the ones who must first submit to God before they can serve in relationships with women. God wants His daughters to be pursued by intentional men and led by godly men leading up to a lifelong marriage covenant.

Before focusing on what to look for in a husband, women must pray to God asking for His wisdom and guidance, asking for His protection and help in making the best choices about any relationship. It is more important to be the right one than to find the right one. God wants women to make sure they love Him first with their heart, mind, soul, and strength (Mark 12:30). This must be done first before any blessings can be received.

Whatever the circumstances that result in women ending up as single parents, God is still faithful. In order to combat the odds against raising children growing up in a one-parent home, they must be guided toward the heavenly Father. If women find themselves raising children alone, then they must trust God to be a "father to the fatherless" (Psalm 68:5). Furthermore, remember that only God can meet all our needs. The need for a Savior is far greater than any earthly comfort or support.

Women must be mindful of their public behavior, modes of dress, attitudes, and actions. They must find their worth and identity in who they are in Christ. Women are beautifully made for men. They ought to embrace fulfilling the Bible's requirements that they are different from men, they are the complement for men, and they have different roles in family and marriage from men. They also must allow Him to utilize them for His specific purpose. Time should be spent expressing the love of God through giving to meet the needs of their husbands, children, and others while taking no concern for themselves. A woman will know that in giving she will receive from God. When this happens, the children will imitate and do likewise. They will marry first, have children, and guide their children towards the Father, and this cycle should continue.

Media Influence

Today we are overly stimulated through the media by television, cell phones, and other electronic devices. We pay too much attention to information that does not matter and not seeing the trace of information that really does matter. News is often like a reality show. It has become mere entertainment. Some of the stories are so redundant that we become s numb hearing them all the time. Media is doing a fantastic job creating a thirst and hunger for scandal, bad news, or the latest trend. We must be mindful that our hearts and mind be protected from subtle manipulation by what we see on a screen (Proverbs 4:23). The impact of today's media to influence human behavior should be a concern for all of us.

Media was designed to deceive the masses, spoon-feed lies to the public, and echo the opinions of corporations. Society is so easy to manipulate through the power of the media. Since the job of the media is to control the information, all they have to do is to devise the situation, create the storyline, make it sound believable and we will fall in the trap and believe it.

These corporations control the media because its multiple outlets are used to sell illusion and delusion to the masses. They also define what is acceptable, what is desirable, and what is not.

Distractions are cleverly designed to draw us away from information that matters. This causes low production and attention spans needed to function in our daily lives. Managing information with distractions is a characteristic of the media such as celebrity news, scandals by public figures, information on the latest technology, and sports. The public is addicted to these topics, craving more of them. These distractions are heavy in coverage but light in content, while more relevant information is seldom covered and considered boring.

Nowadays the media is ramming their own version of what a family looks like down our throats. They have been successful in presenting a multitude of family structures and have promoted the acceptance of alternate family structures. The media has shaped our views of family, God, and men more than we realize. Images of "dumb" fathers, single mothers, stepmothers, and homosexual couples continue to being portrayed in the media. We continue to be taken hostage through hollow and deceptive philosophy, which depends on human tradition based on the principles of this world rather than on Christ (Colossians 2:8).

Where are the shows on TV about a strong nuclear family? Why aren't dads heroes anymore? How about a song about being happily married? Sending a positive message through the media could make wanting a nuclear family cool again. There is no need to always have such poor messages on mainstream media. Yet, the media is churning out more and more programs that directly assault the legitimacy of the nuclear family.

During the early history of television many shows depicted the family as a heterosexual, patriarchal, churchgoing unit with uncorrupted children. Fathers were viewed as breadwinners, heads of families, and respected leaders in the home. Children are now raised in single parent homes with grandparents, in foster homes, or by same-sex parents. Television has the power to shape our morals and values, but many of us do not recognize this. It is also the most powerful medium for creating images about families and fathers.

How fathers are portrayed matters. Today, most dads on TV today are portrayed in the latest sitcoms as the irresponsible, unfaithful, violent abusers or as stupid buffoons with no clue on how to be a parent. Watching television can be sickening when we see how simple-minded and pathetic-looking fathers the male actors are portraying. Some male actors have played roles in which, they need to get in touch with their feminine side by acting or dressing like women. This is an underhanded way of accepting effeminate men on the TV screen, but it is against Scripture in I Corinthians 6:10. Even worse, many shows that focus on families today don't even have an active father role in the storyline. The atmosphere is now created as if fatherhood is no longer important, especially in the eyes of children. This influence by the media on boys can make it difficult for them to aspire to be husbands and fathers or see their own value as fathers. They can retreat to the mode of extended adolescence where there is no commitment or responsibility required of them. This creates a warped view for girls as well. They can be misled into thinking fathers in children's lives aren't important. When things get tough in relationships, these young women grab the mantle of independence where divorce or separation is a viable option and raising children on their own without fathers is a necessity. The Bible remind us to not to be part of these unfruitful works the media is portraying about fatherhood (Ephesians 5:11).

Virtually every program in the media contains greed, materialism, violence, and sexual immorality. In nearly every show they air the Christian faith is devalued. Our eyes and minds are being bombarded on all sides by these programs that generate an insatiable appetite that needs to be satisfied. When exposed to heavy hours of viewing on the screen, boys tend to be influenced by expressing more aggressive behaviors. Girls tend to be influenced by dressing and talking in sexual ways. These behaviors of actors or performers on the screen are glamorized as "normal" behaviors many teens often imitate. This also creates longings to fill voids where boys who do not know how to act as men and girls who long for male attention.

Technology comes with a blessing and a curse at the same time. It has made our lives easier, but it also makes it easier not to connect with others. In today's world, through the power of social media, relationships are artificial, thus creating a false sense of intimacy with others. Social skills using face-to-face communication suffer when there is heavy reliance on technology. Human-to-human relationships have been replaced with human-to-machine relationships. There must be ways to turn off media outlets and to turn on real relationships.

Electronic media is really about narcissism because it is all about wants, deserves, and must-haves, which creates an environment of enjoying the pleasures of this world (Hebrews 11:25). The inability to self-regulate by managing behaviors and emotions are being undermined by participating too much in the virtual world instead of the real world. It is much easier for someone to reach for an electronic device to pass the time than to connect with live people. The behaviors often imitated involve television, movies, video games, and the online world.

The media does a wonderful job of marketing cellular and other electronic devices especially when teens or young adults are the target audience. This feeds into the entitlement and instant gratification behaviors that exist today. Cellular phones, laptops, and other electronic devices have become electronic gods in our lives. Scripture says they must not be the center of attention as idols (Exodus 20:3). We pour all of our personal information into these devices, such as pictures, texts, and phone numbers because the phone does all the work for us.

The Internet has introduced ideas and lifestyles that are often in conflict with parental values. People are connected to anyone in the world through technology. Too much time spent in front of electronic screens is quality time taken away from the family. Parents should be mindful that boys tend to spend time viewing violent or sexual images while girls manage their time posting vicious electronic messages against each other. These issues have created changes in parenting. When was the last time your child's online habits have been monitored? Have you scrolled through texts or swiped through pictures on your teen's cell phone? Changes in parenting happen when parents are too busy and do not know what their children are doing. Parents should never allow their children to be managed or parented by cell phones (I Timothy 3:4).

The battle of relationships between parent and child and the media is difficult enough under any type of family structure. This condition worsens when the father is not in the home. Work schedules and school take time away from basic parent-child interaction. When the father is not present, there is an unquenchable need to fill the void through peers and social media. It also causes them to turn to social media for acceptance and identity. It has become a highly influential teacher for children. Instead of fathers teaching moral, ethical, and biblical values, what is experienced and read on electronic screens are forming values. Social media cannot be used as a tool replacing the void left by fathers.

The media promotes sexuality, violence, and other reckless behaviors; technology gives children access to them. Sexting has become very popular. It includes receiving and sending photo and text messages. Girls tend to do this more often than boys, not realizing the repercussions involving full-blown Internet exposure to pedophiles and law enforcement, causing family embarrassment and tarnished reputations. Proverbs 22:1 discusses the importance of reputations. They are acting with no regard of how much of their bodies they show. A father's influence will not lead children to seek desperate means of attention.

Teens are armed and ready with cell phone cameras to post fights, hoping the video goes viral with high volume of the public viewing them. Sadly, this is a cruel way for young people to network with one another. These fights do not discriminate based on race or environmental location. Sometimes they are staged, sometimes they are in real time, and sometimes the victim is unsuspecting (see Knockout Game). Viewing fighting on videos creates an addiction of fulfilling pleasures of violence through visual stimulation. Media lays the groundwork that degrades the values and behavior of children in society. It is hard to see how fighting can in any way be glorifying to God (I Corinthians 10:31).

A flash mob is considered a type of reckless behavior where the location, place, and time are predetermined. They assemble in a public place, perform random meaningless acts for a brief time, and then quickly scatter. The motives are to get media coverage and simply have pure fun-filled entertainment. Not only do all of these behaviors provide instant gratification and pleasurable escapes, but they also provides children with courage to act them out through texts, posts, or videos in order to gain an audience's attention and a following. If anyone is overexposed to sex, violence, and reckless behaviors for a significant period of time, then it can lead to attraction to and imitation of these behaviors. God does not want our youth to fall into demonic traps of this world but to be fine examples of believers (I Timothy 4:12).

Music culture, in a lot of ways, has replaced parenting because of its ability to manipulate the hearts and minds of the youth. Unfortunately, the music industry has come to fill in that void left by the father. Boys and girls alike are constantly searching for that role model. The music industry continues to influence the artists to shape the mindset of our youth by endorsing rape, murder, forced sex, sadomasochism, adultery, and satanic worship in its lyrics. What has become popular with the youth is really going overboard with satanic lyrics and sexual gyrating antics on videos. The key to listening to any form of music is in its message and purpose.

Constant attention to technology makes it very difficult to make time for God. All types of recreational leisure have become idols when our needs must be met through with music, television, movies, videos, computers, and concerts. Idol worshipping of celebrities and athletes is commonplace. People are willing to stand in lines for hours buying their products or being entertained by them. There are people who entertain guests with "watch parties" to idolize their favorite athlete or celebrity. Let us not forget He is a jealous God. This means God will not tolerate mankind worshipping and bowing down to other gods or idols other than Himself (Exodus 20:3).

We have become connected and disconnected with one another at the same time. Most people are afraid to get deeper and connect. On one hand we are connected in the electronic world through social media, emails, videos, and texts. However, on the other hand, our social skills are inept because there is no connection face to face. There must be a balance between connecting with the real world and the virtual world. We were created for relationship, not isolation. Even God stated that is not good for man to be alone (Genesis 2:18). This situation worsens when fathers aren't around to connect with their families.

It is truly amazing how media technology impact our lives in a relatively short amount of time. Internet, social media, and cell phones are some Satan's greatest weapons that hinder our mindset on things rather than on God. It's relatively easy to get seduced by the pleasures technology has to offer because it makes everything so simple and easy to get ahold of. Technology in itself is not bad. All of us can enjoy the blessings and pleasures of this life without being mastered by them. Internet, social media, and cell phone usage should be a safety concern for all of us, and we must be mindful of how it affects us daily.

Society generates perverted content through the media that degrades family values. There are biblical guidelines for dealing with the sex, greed, and violence that permeate the media today. We must be mindful of its traps when we live self-centered lifestyles and succumb to mindless pleasures. We must first be connected to the right source (John 15:5). Not all media is corruptible. There are a few media outlets bringing the Good News of the Gospel, although the channels are not as plentiful as secular ones. Eventually we must choose either to be molded by the media or to serve our Creator.

Media is a powerful communication channel that is able to twist and distort God's truth as being either repulsive or oppressive. In other words, the Word of God is viewed by some as limiting our freedom of human thought or action. Jesus said in Scriptures the only way to the Father is to go through Him (John 14:6). We must guard ourselves against confusion, distortions, and distractions that the media is designed to do. Media routinely degrades fathers and manipulates children with technology. God does not care about how much you enjoy entertainment. He wants us to love Him, serve Him, and obey His commandments (John 14:15).

Impact the Community

Fatherlessness is the engine driving our most urgent social problems in our communities. There are a lot of problems in our communities including out-of-wedlock births, criminal delinquent behaviors, gangs, poverty, child support and welfare policies, unemployment, and mass incarceration. These issues start a chain of negative events eventually leading to more government involvement. Although these issues are many, they still lead to the same source—the absence of a father. A father not in the home is directly responsible for the ills in a given community. There is nothing more devastating in our homes, communities, or lives than a father who is absent.

The biggest problem in our communities begins with the breakdown of the family. Since the Garden of Eden the war against the family has been raging, and the casualties have been high (Genesis 3: 1–7). Fatherless families are the single largest source of poverty. Society views the problem with poverty as simply a black issue, which could not be further from the truth. It's really a human sin issue based on choices, decisions, and circumstances. More than half of all newborn babies are entering into the world without a nuclear family in place. There are dire consequences for children born into nonmarital homes.

When entire neighborhoods are dominated by fatherless families, then that community is asking for and getting chaos. Any community with a large number of children to grow up in homes dominated by women, never acquiring a stable relationship with a positive male role model, is a recipe for disaster. Large concentrations of single parent families in any given community increases the odds of boys being involved in crime and girls becoming pregnant. It is possible for children to sidestep these potential negative outcomes and live successful and productive lives. However, even being raised by the strongest well-meaning single mother does not prevent children from becoming single moms or absent dads.

Conditions of neighborhoods, schools, and local businesses are directly impacted by homes without fathers. They play significant roles in shaping lives of each generation by affecting them directly and indirectly. Seeking worldly pleasures always takes away something without ever giving back anything. Nothing substitutes for God (I Timothy 2:5–6). The social role of fathers has been diminished and devalued fatherhood has led to more suffering in our communities.

Destructive social issues are everywhere, but they seem to be pervasive in communities with high concentration of single parent families. These issues may include higher incidences of crime, chemical dependency, domestic violence, child sexual abuse, and child poverty. Living near power plants and landfills cause longtime exposure to lead, mercury, water and air pollution, and food deserts lead to a host of health problems. We are to do good to our neighbors, and Scripture reminded us that all of the people on this Earth are our neighbors (Galatians 6:10).

Satan uses an array of arsenals at his disposal to destroy families. The government uses lawyers, social service agencies, and courtrooms ready, willing, and able to pry families apart. Law enforcement officials are on standby to arrest children in schools or on the streets. Unemployment creates destructive options of acquiring income through illegal or sexual means for daily living purposes. There seems to be a serious crusade against fathers in destroying marriages, undermining parents, and ruining the lives of children.

Local businesses are important to the financial stability in the community. Once there is an increase in crime, businesses either close their doors forever or more move to neighborhoods with a stronger economical financial base. This creates changes in the clientele. When businesses are owned by people who do not live in the community, all the money made leaves the community. The tax dollars leave with the business shrinking the tax base. This in turn causes the local economy in the neighborhood to suffer financially. Once businesses lose emotional attachments to their neighborhoods, the community suffers. Neighborhood deterioration begins when high-end or middle-end stores are replaced with low-end stores.

Our communities are arranged by income, by social and economic status, and by the kind of work we do. Minimum wage jobs may be livable for one person but not a family of four. Limited income reduces the ability to choose neighborhoods to bring children up in safer and more productive economic surroundings. Unfortunately, income determines accessibility in living in communities where there is decent housing, transportation, quality schools, safe streets and parks, and healthy food stores.

Unfortunately dysfunctional families are the rule rather than the exception in many communities without fathers. Who is going to help lift the mother when she is shouldering the burden of raising the family alone? This is where the government starts assuming their role as protector and provider in the home. Protection provided by the power of courts, social agencies, and police against fathers and providers is the power to collect alimony or child support payments from fathers. Provision of financial assistance is also given to support mothers and children. The cost of family unit breakdown is paid by all taxpayers especially when there are children involved.

Laws created by government have helped contribute to fatherlessness and family destruction. Current polices promote women having nearly any man except the biological father heading the house. This encourages cohabitation, single parenting, and out-of-wedlock births. When government replaces fathers as provider in the home, the men would be eventually forced to leave their family. The Bible warns us of those who help create division in families (Matthew 12:25). The Bible speaks against family disintegration through these means.

Our court system creates the assumption that mothers should have more rights than fathers. For divorce or unwed fathers, many men argue that family courts send the message that fatherhood is not as important as motherhood. The court system is pushing fathers away from their children's lives, redefining marriage from its traditional definition of one man and one woman and making fathers merely an option. They rationalize that the discrimination against fathers is justified "in the best interest of the child." Fathers are only good enough to spend their paychecks in exchange for the weekend visits with their children. The message given to fathers is that they are invisible or irrelevant in their children's lives, unless it involves financial support, which makes them somewhat visible.

The penal system has contributed to fatherlessness. Prisons are full of people who were abandoned by their fathers. This vicious cycle eliminates fathers, and the lives of children are sacrificed. As long as the norm in communities is for boys and men to father children without raising them, the number of prisoners will continue to increase. Even though these numbers are constantly growing, it seems more and more people do not fear punishment for crimes committed. We will all be given an account before God when this life is over (Romans 14:12).

The breakdown of the family and removing God from schools go hand in hand. Banning prayer in schools has led to the moral decline of this fallen world. Antisocial behaviors of verbal taunts, fighting, and cyber bullying are common in school settings. Schools districts are forced to come up with programs that involve restoration and restitution to deal with disruptive, defiant behaviors. More and more programs are squeezed in the seven-hour school day to combat behaviors, yet test scores and overall achievement are still on the decline.

There seems to be an explosion of sexual behavior in schools as well, especially in the electronic cyber arena. Children are introduced to sex too soon; they are forced to grow up without anyone's permission or protection. As stated from the previous chapter, sexting or posting sexually suggestive images seems to be common among teens. This leads to children engaging in irresponsible sex and having children they cannot take care of, thus creating a continuous dysfunctional cycle of young single mothers and young fathers who abandoned their responsibility and leave. Mentoring programs are available, but restoration of fathers with God as the foundation is a far better solution.

Schools are becoming more of breeding ground for young criminals. Children growing up in fatherless households are at a greater risk for experiencing learning disorders, behavioral problems, and interpersonal aggression in schools. The blatant disrespect of teachers, parents, peers, and other authority figures are certainly common in most schools. Many of them are placed in special education classes. Oppositional defiant behaviors are controlled with police presence and alternative programs. These are clear signs that we are in the latter days. Scripture says, *"For men will be lovers of themselves, lovers of money, boasters, proud, blasphemers, disobedient to parents . . ."* (2 Timothy 3:2). Schools recognize the differences with involved fathers whose presence exudes authority and discipline. There is recognition on part of educators where they identify the unique contributions that fathers make on students' behavior and academic achievement.

A powerful force for children, especially boys, is the need to belong to a family or group. Children are genetically wired for connection with others. Children want to belong to something they can believe in, something they can call family. They will begin to look outside the home for connections. When hopelessness settles in from dysfunction of family life, this is where drugs, alcohol, or gangs are easy influences.

Oftentimes, they turn to this destructive lifestyle because there is no father spending time, giving direction, and showing love to them. The modeling of roles and behavior from a father is absent. Anger is built up during the critical years of childhood, and it's channeled through violence against people or property. When validation is not present, then people will start looking on the outside for it. Gangs can be found in most communities across the country.

Across the globe, millions of young men and women are caught up in gangs. When fathers are absent and mothers are always working, it gives children idle time with no guidance. Gangs provide a sense of purpose with a certain reputation plus attractive benefits such as protection, job security regardless of the economy, and even access to revenge. This gives children an attractive combination of things organizations and families cannot offer. The Bible clearly states about not being enticed to this type of opportunity (Proverbs 1:10).

Social issues from dysfunctional neighborhoods decrease nonresident fathers' involvement with their children. It is unfortunate that so many young people have given up on society because of obstacles they face. They believe that in order to escape from poverty, they must get into sports or the entertainment business. Others will join the culture of drugs and crime as a means of survival. Those who engage in violence have seen it from their homes and neighborhoods. Behaviors from these barriers are copied and become a way of life passed on to the next generation. Children growing up without fathers have often struggled to deal with their emotions.

Communities without fathers leading families cause chaos, confusion, and calamity. Although deterioration of communities did not happen overnight, it will take a significant amount of time to restore them. Keys of triggering transformation in communities must include inclusion of fathers, restoration of businesses, employment with livable wages, schools with ample resources, and an increase in church membership. As a community we must encourage each other, build each other up, and strive for the betterment for God's kingdom. God want us to dwell together in unity (Psalm 133:1).

When it comes to restoration of our communities, we must return to the biblical standard God is holding us to in order to resolve issues in our families. The foundation of everything must be rooted in sound Biblical principles (II Timothy 2:19). Changing family structure by being married families is a great place to start. Marriage is supposed to provide a vehicle for husbands and wives taking care of each other, raising the next generation, and maintaining stable communities. Marriage itself does not completely eliminate poverty or reduce crime in our communities, but it is a far better option than unmarried families.

Whether you are a father, stepfather, grandfather, uncle, or adoptive parent, fathers are an important factor in the development of our children and community. We have failed to nurture the communities God has given us. Men are charged with the responsibility to tend to and keep communities intact. It will take their real leadership in rebuilding marriages, families, neighborhoods, and communities. They will be the catalyst of strength and maintain relationships in the community. In order for us to rebuild our communities, we must be recommitted to God (Psalm 37:5).

Our mindset must be transformed in order to show love and compassion to others. We must be united together to overcome Satan's influence and power over our communities. However, by the way we live our lives, we have become more isolated and care more about ourselves than others. We lost compassion and love for our neighbors. When Jesus walked the earth, there are two commandments he gave: Love God with all of your heart, soul and mind. Love your neighbors as yourself (Matthew 22:36–40). Turning our hearts and minds as a community back to Him is a great start in resolving social issues of out-of-wedlock births, criminal delinquent behaviors, gangs, poverty, shady policies and laws, unemployment, and mass incarceration in our communities.

Do Ye Church?

We must remember that the church is the people, not the building. Can the building fellowship, worship, and preach? Of course not! Everything is carried out by people, not buildings (I Corinthians 3:9). People have come together to praise and glorify God outside, in homes, under tents, in schools, and at other buildings with or without crosses and stained-glass windows. We often lose sight that we are the church. Scripture says we are the body of Christ (I Corinthians 12:27). Yet, the threat to the freedom of worshipping the risen Christ is a threat to Christians everywhere in the world.

Questions must be examined when it comes to male membership in churches. What topics are being covered from the pulpit? Why is Jesus portrayed only as meek and mild? Is the ambiance of the church building appealing to both genders? What types of songs does the choir sing? How often does the collection plate or basket come out? Why are services too long, anyway? Isn't the preacher just a man? These rhetorical questions create reasons as to why men don't attend church.

Fathers attending local churches are key factors in keeping young people from falling away from their faith. When earthly fathers are not involved, then it is very difficult for young people to believe in the heavenly Father. It is very difficult for fathers instructing the ways of the world from a biblical standpoint to their children when they are not present. Churches must improve on helping young people connect with God and to build ministries appealing to boys and girls. This falling away would lead young people to stop attending local churches, abandon the faith, and follow their own humanistic ideology (I Timothy 4:1).

We live in a society today that diminishes the role of men, discounts the importance of fathers, and dismisses the male gender as disposable and unnecessary. When you have fatherless homes in fatherless communities, then expect the local churches to be fatherless as well. A mindset the church has adopted is that the father is of little use in the home and in the lives of children. The majority of local churches are full of children, mothers, and elderly members. A sad reality is the majority of men attending church hold a leadership position: pastor, deacon, trustee, or usher.

There is a gaping hole of men between ages of eighteen to thirty in churches. Whom does this age group look to as role models? Who teaches young men how to be good husbands, fathers, and workers? Who will help young women to look beyond the surface of men when they are pursued as prospective girlfriends, wives, and mothers? The best source to address these questions is found in the Bible. II Timothy 3:16–17 states, *"All Scripture is given by inspiration of God, and is profitable for doctrine, for reproof, for correction, for instruction in righteousness, that the man of God may be complete, thoroughly equipped for every good work."* Churches are doing a poor job of being relevant in reaching out in the lives of these young men.

A father's commitment to the Christian faith is a determining factor whether or not children remain in church as adults. Generally speaking, if fathers don't attend church, their children are far less likely to attend church. When fathers stop going to church, they teach their children, especially boys, that church isn't really that important and the word of God does not hold much value. If there is no father, then mothers, grandmothers, and Sunday school teachers are delegated the upbringing of their children to the church.

Church is an institution where the development of values and morals are cultivated. A biological father's presence in the church is probably the most important factor of leading his family to Christ as opposed to the mighty influence of the world. When families don't read the Bible and pray together, then the Scriptures are not valued. Nothing is unsettling for anyone to choose between the conflicting parallels of the Word of God versus the laws of the land (Acts 5:29).

Parents who are believers want their children to spend eternity in heaven. Therefore, the children must be shown examples of righteous living, which is showing them Jesus Christ in the Bible every day (I Corinthians 11:1). God placed this responsibility on the fathers. Fathers do matter, and their influence and participation in church attendance and the spiritual development of their children is a great indicator of how successful families are at passing their faith on to the next generation. It is very interesting to note children's attendance is higher when the father is regular and the mother is irregular and when both parents are regular.

This information regarding church attendance proves why God set the father as the spiritual head of the family. God's grace and mercy makes it possible for children still grow up to become mature Christian adults, even when their parents miss the mark in this area.

Church has developed a culture that is driving men away. Has the metaphor "Bride of Christ" been literally taken a bit too far? The perception is the church's music, ministries, and messages cater to women. A close examination of the choir will show its membership is mostly women. Praise dancing and praise songs are endearing to women, not men. The lyrics of the songs seemed to be more intimate and less vigorous. Women must feel secure, and men must be challenged. There must be a balance with being secure and being challenged to accomplish a task for Christ.

Ministries are female-centered while men are on the bottom of the totem pole. Women have Bible studies, prayer groups, support groups, teas, and retreats and, of course, children have a plethora of programs. There are also nursing, hospitality, and cooking ministries where women have ample opportunity to serve. Men may have an annual men's day which pretty much sums up men's ministries. More ministries and activities need to be created for men to utilize their skills to be of service. Once men feel their contribution for service is not necessary, they will withdraw, disconnect, and leave the church.

Churches tend to teach and preach on the "feel good" sermons of salvation and forgiveness and not of enough "tough love" sermons of sin and persecution. II Timothy 3:16 reminds us that teaching from all of the Scriptures is vitally important for living. Sometimes there are sermons that guilt churchgoers into giving money, which can make it hard to differentiate the hustlers on the street from the hustlers behind the pulpit. During any given sermon there will be shouting, hand-raising, crying, and swaying, which are outward emotions common to women. Sermons must be engaging to both men and women in the church. These are some of the reasons why men stay away from church. These reasons make men cynical and distrusting of the church. Do we need to bring the men to church or the church to men?

Oftentimes, the church destroys its own wounded better than anyone by simply handing the weapons to the enemy. Instead of offering hope and healing, churches inflict more injury. It is not supposed to be a house of saints but a place where sinners are openly welcomed. It seems we have saints while in the church but cowards when they leave outside those four walls. Large sums of money go into the building have no impact on the surrounding neighborhood. Church members exercise their right to remain silent about the Gospel to people on the "outside." What have churches done to draw men to church instead of pushing them away from church? A call to local churches is needed to fill the gap with men and to impact the surrounding community for lifeline and stability. If churches want to begin filling that gap, then the issue of fatherlessness must be addressed in pulpits.

Even today, it is rare for a church to publically cry aloud against the evils of sexual immorality. Why are the churches silent? Isaiah 58:1 reminds us to publicly cry out against anything that rebels against God. Most churches will not address this issue of fornication, which in most instances leads to single parenting, same-sex parenting, and grandparent parenting. A vicious generational cycle of random sex that produces consequences of unplanned pregnancy, sexually transmitted diseases, and fatherlessness continues to rage on.

We act as though if sexuality is not discussed, it will go away. Some families have secrets that have been carefully swept under the rug for no one to ever discover. Countless people in the church have their purpose or destiny altered because of sexual sins (remember Abraham and Hagar in Genesis 16). The truth is, so many adult children and their children are still being punished for the sins of their fathers.

Other uncovered topics from the pulpit are a problem that grows in silence. Some topics include addictions, cohabitation, mental illness, domestic violence, or women in pulpits. Could it be the reason for many of these topics are not covered is because those in church leadership are wrestling with some of these sins and are in too deep with the flesh and not in the spirit? Is there worry of pushback from those in the pews if biblical principles are applied to the issues of the day? The inability for churches to stand against perversions and hypocrisy as unaddressed issues does not align with the will of God. Therefore, fear of losing tax-exempt status, membership, and money are more logical reasons as to why controversial topics are not regularly preached. However, these topics are sorely needed to be heard in the congregation and are commissioned by the Lord (II Timothy 2:15).

Father's Day sermons are another topic many men, especially men of color, take an annual beating. Preaching about on this topic can reopen wounds they tried to heal and restore memories they tried to erase. These memories of their father can become painful instead of happy. These sermons can reinforce the concept of men being weak and women being the more spiritual gender. This of course, is not true and not even supported biblically. The church must offer some people a relationship with a perfect heavenly Father who does no wrong. Every good and perfect gift comes from Him. Even though earthly fathers may change, our heavenly Father does not change (Micah 3:6).

The decline of Christianity has directly led to a giant increase in societal sins, including destruction of families, lost morality, and corrupted values. A corrupt system, dominated by anti-Christian groups, is forcing citizens into lives of dependency from the government and not on Christ. Once churches receive money from any governmental agency or utilizing the (501c3) tax codes; then the state becomes the head not Jesus Christ. They are restrained from preaching against government policies and laws that conflict with the

Word of God such as abortion, homosexuality, false teachings, and many others. This is further explained in Galatians 5:19–21.

Satan is continuing in an attack mode by destroying local churches. He knows if there is an attack on families in the church, then there is a great chance of destroying the church. So what are churches doing to address this pressing problem? The word of God is muzzled by the red tape of governmental bureaucracy. These restrictions have a strong influence on fatherlessness but also are used as an instrument to control family life. True Christianity cannot be confined behind to the four walls of any church.

God chose the concept of family relationships to communicate His relationship to us. The term *Father* describes His relationship to us as his children. In John 3:16, Jesus is referred to as God's only begotten Son. Apostle Paul was a great example of fatherhood to his spiritual son, Timothy, in ministry. There are other examples throughout the Bible with examples of fatherhood. It takes men and families building relationships with children and young adults intentionally looking for spiritual sons and daughters to adopt unofficially.

Young people who find themselves in this situation should look at others for examples of fatherhood. They have never experienced the loving grace of an earthly father and because of this absence, they struggle to understand the deep void they feel for a heavenly Father as well. There are some men who demonstrate great examples of fatherhood. These examples must include positive honorable traits and should be incorporated into their own personality and character. Teachable moments based on biblical principles will be given as opportunities for growth by gaining wisdom through time and observation. Even in this fallen world, it is very difficult to find a strong role model for fathers.

Never before was witnessed in this time of history where men are driven far away from the local church. There seems to be disconnection between the moral decay of society and the importance of the church. The curse of fatherlessness in modern society is but a mere reflection of the lack of fathering in the church. Men must return to step in the forefront by leading in their homes and church. Women are needed in the background to provide support instead of expressing a desire to step in just to get the job done

Our culture has dumbed down the importance and difference between masculinity and femininity. Bible states that we are created male and female (Genesis 1:27). Each one is equal in creation and salvation in the sight of God but with different roles and responsibilities. The differences in functional gender roles does not equate to lack of importance, value, or quality between them. God is the one who assigns roles and functions for men and women in family structure and church. This can be further explained in I Corinthians 11:3: *"But I want you to know that the head of every man is Christ, the head of woman is man, and the head of Christ is God."*

God is not the author of confusion (I Corinthians 14:33), but the world has done its job of turning the church into something men perceive as a place for women and children only. Every man needs a father. Every man craves the love, acceptance, and approval of a father. Chances are when men are walking into your church doors, they are fatherless, both spiritually and literally. The problem is many of these young men are without fathers who are faithful in guiding them or other male role models who offer inspiration and instruction. Satan is continuing an attack mode in this area; what are churches doing to address this pressing problem? The church should be a vital part of a ministry that reaches out to these men.

Churches must be cognizant of how they structure their service. It is very difficult for men to follow church leaders who do not exhibit high quality characteristics differ from their own. Every leader must demonstrate a lifestyle consistent with the moral standards of Scripture (Titus 1:5–9). They must have the knack to speak about who men really are and what men need to grow spiritually, emotionally, and financially. If services are structured correctly, then not only will they will reach men, but woman and children also.

Jesus showed us how to grow a healthy church by focusing on men first. He is the founder and the foundation of the church as it was told to Peter (Matthew 16:18). Christ loved women and children, but he spent most of his time and energy developing a handful of men. He knew that when men are transformed, their families, their communities, and their nations will also be transformed. When churches reach out to men, their family will follow.

Churches have become focused on their institution rather than their mission. Arguments follow when churches changes their customs, traditions, or history. We often lose sight when we fail to see the difference between God's commands and man's traditions. Churches must be dedicated to preaching the whole Word of God knowing that the Bible's primary agenda is the salvation of the world through Jesus Christ.

The value of eternal life must outweigh the life of this fallen world. Churches are weak and in decline because church members have lost the biblical understanding of what it means to be part of the body of Christ. Nevertheless, the local church is not called to be masculine or feminine. We are called to be faithful in spreading the Gospel through the salvation of Jesus Christ. If it is faithful, the local church will be attractive to those whom God is calling, fathers or not.

Final Remarks

The moral collapse of society is a direct attack on the family unit. Fatherlessness is the repercussion for civilization from reaping of sins sown by parents (Galatians 6:7). As stated many times before, fatherlessness is the consequence with sin as its root. So many sins are encouraged and even celebrated. Everything God has created must be established as the foundation with the family as the building block for all human relationships.

Fatherlessness has a direct impact on a child's life. Boys are angry and confused because their fathers are not there to mold them into the men God desire for them to be. Girls want to be loved and cherished, but without fathers in their lives, they are looking for love in all of the wrong places. Mass media has created an impression of fathers as being oversexed, abusive, dumb Neanderthals, thus, making fatherhood an afterthought. Fatherlessness has turned our communities into poor crime-ridden warzones whether it is urban, suburban, or rural. Our local churches are having a difficult time in reaching strong viable men to the congregation so they can be fit for spiritual leadership in their families.

Family Affair Recap

Fatherlessness is spreading like a plague in every corner of the world. It operates like a family tsunami with its far-reaching generational consequences. As of 2014, over 70 percent of the children born to a black mother do not live with their father; Hispanic children (55%) are close behind, and Caucasian children are near the 40 percent mark. Fatherlessness is not only an American problem; it is a global problem. Currently, most of the thirty-plus countries researched are allies of the United States. There are not enough researchers to investigate or monitor this epidemic in other countries around the world. Most news outlets will report on murders, wars, and the economy but not the issue of fatherlessness. To usher in the anti-Christ in this fallen world, the rapid declining pace of fatherlessness must continue.

Sin has a devastating effect on families. A true definition of a broken home is when God is not in the equation as the foundation for the family and the failure to recognize him as Savior. Obviously there are no homes that are perfect, no matter what type of family structure exist there. There are cases where children are born to homes of nuclear families who dropped out of school, abused drugs, and became involved in the penal system. No family can cast a safety net to prevent all the dangers of life.

We should know that the whole world is under the control of the evil one (I John 5:19). Satan, with the help of specific interest groups and secular systems, are using their ungodly viewpoints and principles to pass laws and policies aimed at the traditional family. It is a bilking scheme to siphon money out of families, generate revenue, and destroy families in the process. Divorce is easy to file, courts prevent fathers' custody and visitation rights, tax laws penalize marriages, and out-of-wedlock births are rewarded financially.

When the fathers have resigned, mothers are redefined, children are maligned, and God is undermined. Not only does this make the family structure unbalanced, but more importantly, it shifts away from God's divine order. A destructive domino effect happens when the father is removed from the family through any and all means. Systems are in place for implementation of the agenda for the planned destruction of our families.

Society gives the message that traditional marriage is outdated, and that virtually any family form, including out-of-wedlock parenthood, is acceptable. One man and one woman are viewed as antiquated even though God created mankind in that specific order. Broken marriages always involve at least one partner moving away from God. As soon as Adam and Eve disobeyed God, there was division in the marriage from each other, and Adam began pointing the finger at Eve for his problems. Marriage is God's excellent perfect plan that every child needs a mother and a father.

God has given us specific instructions in His word about how we are to live together as families. Even though specific roles are set, these do not mean inequality between husband and wife. We tend to forget we were not designed to live for ourselves, but rather for His purpose and design. Self-help and other manmade solutions to human problems generally only scratch the surface. However, the power from Scriptures can reach deeper in our hearts and have granted us everything we need pertaining to life (II Peter 2:13).

Lost Boys Recap

Many boys are finding very few examples of what authentic fatherhood, manhood, and family structure look like. They model false manhood behaviors from peers because fathers were not present to teach how to act like men. These men must be able to lead from the front and not from the back as Adam did. The absence of these examples has also impacted the rate at which nuclear families are being created. Fatherhood is as redemptive as God the Father redeemed us in Jesus Christ the Son like the Prodigal Son Parable in Luke 15. The most integral part of any parent-child relationship is the father-son relationship. This connection is crucial for a couple of reasons: headship and lineage.

Society has not made it easy for men who desire sex. We live in a culture in which divorce, infidelity, promiscuity, and cohabitation are prevalent and invariably affect the way men relate to women. Many of them view young women primarily as a means of sexual gratification. Boys will imitate their absent fathers by not fulfilling basic parenting responsibilities; therefore, they will grow up in a world where it is perfectly normal for them to conceive children and then disappear from those children's lives. Men are held accountable by God for the condition of the family (I Corinthians 11:3).

Fathers did teach their sons a few things. So what did fathers who are not present in the lives of their sons actually teach them? Leave the responsibility of raising children to mothers. A child support or welfare check is actually taking care of the child/children. Fathers taught sons not to pray because they can do it all by themselves. Fathers also taught their sons how to be selfish because they can spend time with whomever and whatever they choose to do. God said to fathers over and over again to teach the children (Deuteronomy 11:19).

We should be concerned with the agenda of depopulation in this fallen world. Boys are not finishing high school, and young men not finishing college. Men are unable to find work or stay employed and are not committing to marriages. There are now more single people than married people. When fathers are removed from the family, their authority and discipline are also removed. Every man must examine himself to determine if his legacy is left with an inheritance or heritage.

Girls Gone Wild Recap

A father is the first man that a little girl wants to please. Girls understand how a woman should be treated by the way their fathers treat their mothers. The development of self-confidence and self-esteem are key ingredients for positive relationships fathers can impart on their daughters. General concerns of body image and self-centeredness by girls would be less of an issue. Girls, in relationships with their fathers, would be reminded of their worth and how much they are truly valued.

Family breakdown and fatherlessness in particular are wreaking havoc on our society. Many women allow men to enter their presence and their essence by fulfilling a role of a wife to men who are not their husband. They often are involved in dysfunctional relationships with emotionally unavailable, uncommitted men subconsciously by reverting back to the behaviors of their absent fathers. Women must be savvy enough not to be intimate with someone until he meets the criteria of husband and father. Material quantity must not be pursued in place of character quality. Women must be willing to be led by marrying a husband not a boyfriend (Ephesians 5:23).

When Satan wants to destroy society, he begins to attack the family with the woman. Everything reverts back to Genesis 3 where Satan went to the woman. Satan convinced Eve that her way was better than God's. She tried to be independent of her husband. She seized Adam's responsibility in leadership and was deceived. The conflict of the sexes was born out of the fall in the Garden of Eden. Women would desire to rule over men, but men would instead rule (Genesis 3:15–16).

A new definition of womanhood needs to be defined that includes the love of God, men, and children. They must first trust in the Lord and reject society's belief that anything or anyone else can satisfy those needs (Proverbs 3:5–6). Women must not only believe in but follow God's plan, know their role, and complement her husband's responsibilities to make relationships and marriages work. However, they do not have to be married or be mothers to serve those in need. They must ultimately be true in all well-doing regardless of where she presently is in life, to the honor and glory of God by honoring His Word. True womanhood is not about altering physical appearance or the ability to bring forth life. It is about allowing God to use women in fulfilling His purpose to bring Him glory.

Media Influence Recap

All over the world Christians are being jailed, tortured, and murdered for the sake of their faith. Eventually, this act of violence will reach the Western part of the world. The Christian faith is relentlessly mocked, ridiculed, and demonized on television, in the movies, and on the Internet. We have witnessed laws and policies that are anti-Christian in nature regularly being passed.

Something's terribly wrong with the whole system of bad behavior being rewarded by way of electronic media. Big corporations use television that tells-a-vision through programs of what to buy, how to behave, or what to believe. These companies will try anything to cut corners, boost sales, or buy and sell products for the purpose of profit, no matter the consequences. Corporations are in the business with these two things in mind: control and profit. It is a powerful psychological warfare. Ephesians 6:12 warns us of spiritual wickedness in high places. These programs are designed to persuade and influence our perception on fatherhood as being useless and unnecessary.

The attitudes and beliefs of children about fatherhood correlate with the amount of television watched. It is easy for them to believe fathers behave like the ones in the media. Parents must monitor what children are watching and how much they are watching.

Parents are competing with media for the battle of their children's relationships. Too much time is spent on devices rather than with one another. Ever consider making time for God as part of the equation? The lack of communication causes children to turn to electronic gadgets where they are facing obstacles, uncertainty about issues, or fears of rejection in their lives. Media-free zones must be enforced to maintain the basic parent-child relationship. A great place for this to start is at the dinner table.

Impact the Community Recap

We often cry out after a mass shooting in public places or stray bullets killing our children. Simply increasing the presence of police everywhere a crime is possible does little to identify and solve the real social problem. The downside to a police state is limiting basic freedoms of its citizens. Where are the parents of those pulling the trigger? How much of an impact did they have in their upbringing? Even though God hears us when we cry out to Him, I believe God stopped hearing our cries because we stopped hearing Him (Psalm 145:19).

Broken homes and the collapse of the nuclear family create chaotic conditions in communities. As a result, schools are underfunded, unemployment rates are high, and thriving businesses leave the community. This is a direct outcome of fathers being absent from the homes and lives of their children. Many people are murdered, robbed, and raped by fatherless children when they grow older. Cemeteries and jail complexes are filled up by men, especially those of color. This is often reported as a black issue, but in truth, it is not restricted to black families.

Our communities need be restored and turned back to God. We must stop surrendering to the wicked and relinquishing our neighborhoods. Building families with fathers leading them is a key step in restoration. We can empower youth to take pride in their communities.

Employment, mentoring, and enrichment programs would help them be more responsible youth. Programs of premarital education would stress the importance of marriage in child-rearing. This will aid in the ability for everyone to live in the neighborhood without fear of anyone or anything. Obviously, this will take a long period of time to implement or even difficult to start up since people are not willing to do the work (Matthew 9:37).

Do Ye Church Recap

Many churches stood on the sidelines and watched all of this happen or worse, participated and perpetuated the issue of fatherlessness. The silence from the pulpit on this problem is deafening. The lack of men in the church is a concern, but the conditions of our hearts should be a greater concern.

Satan has wonderfully set up a system where it is very difficult for preachers to speak against any wrongdoings of government, people, secret places, or anything else with opposing viewpoints to the Word of God. They offer the carrot of tax-exempt status dangling over the heads of the local churches in order to significantly restrict what can be said in pulpits across America.

Unfortunately some preachers are watering down the gospel in order to avoid offending people. They are not supposed to be ashamed of the gospel but will speak the truth without fear (II Timothy 2:15). This is a turn-off for men, because the sermons are not challenging enough with a goal in mind. Local churches must include teachings of sin and hell and the dangers of not following Jesus Christ.

It is disheartening to witness men who are Muslims and Jehovah Witnesses unafraid to walk through neighborhoods, even the poverty-stricken, crime-ridden ones. Yet in Christian churches the few men there are remain huddled inside their buildings, not reaching out to the people to share the Gospel in surrounding communities. People are clapping, singing, and shouting *inside* the walls of the local church, but what impact are they having *outside* the walls of the church?

Conclusion

Today, society at large rejects the idea of God and Christianity. Absolute truth is being abandoned. There is a morality shift away from God because of our sinful behavior. Society is built upon having more even though Jesus said his grace is sufficient (II Corinthians 12:9). We believe in our own thinking, we get what we want, and we cling to our own emotions. Pride fills up so much of our lives leaving no room for God (Psalms 10:4). Sinful behavior is accepted because it has been defended, tolerated, excused, and explained away by many people. God is being systematically removed from all aspects of society across the globe.

Society tells us we must accept everything and be open-minded or not judge someone. We even go as far as believing in something false through various communication means in order to make it true. This is the classic definition of rational lies (rationalize). Ephesians 5:6 reminds us, "Let no one deceive you with empty words, for because of these things the wrath of God comes upon the sons of disobedience." Sometimes we have to act in a manner contrary to what others may believe. The goal of

Satan is to pervert the Word with lies, invert gender roles, and subvert the relationship with God by our turning away from Him. All of us want to be loved, cherished, protected, and valued. These are specific traits fathers can provide. It is very reasonable these days for children living without fathers. Unfortunately, there are times when earthly fathers fail to fulfill their role. Only God can finish the duty as Father where men have stopped. Let us not forget that God is the creator of fatherhood.

Every decision, good or bad, has consequences. Mankind likes the broad, easy way, which leads to violence, wars, earthquakes, floods, fires, hurricanes, and tornadoes instead of the narrow straight way leading to eternal life (Matthew 7:14). We can see what happens in the lives of people who disregard God's Word. Don't ever be fooled into thinking that your actions don't have consequences. Don't think you can get away with bad choices even if you don't seem to get caught. As we age it is easier to see the choices people make when they're younger, but many of the consequences they reap from those decisions are when they are older.

The enemy is intentional in opposing God and destroying all God does. We must make decisions that honor the Lord and agree with the Scriptures. A reminder in Matthew 10:32–33 states, *"Therefore whoever confesses Me before men, him I will also confess before My Father who is in heaven. But whoever denies Me before men, him I will also deny before My Father who is in heaven."* Let us continue to stand on it and for it.

People in society may change, culture may change, but the word of God does not change. These attitudes of the heart are evidenced in making a choice to rebel against God's standard for obedience because it's so desperately wicked (Jeremiah 17:9). Many people aren't willing to change what they love to do in their lives when it can be called out Biblically. Scripture also says in Malachi 3:6 *"For I am the Lord, I change not . . ."*

God loves all people but hates the sin. God is "anti-sin," no matter how it is expressed. He comes to us with outstretched arms, and wants us to turn away from sin and establish a relationship with Him. The good news is that it is never too late to make a change. God forgives sin, but we must stop committing sinful acts (I John 3:6).

No matter what happens in this world, God is still in control. There is nothing new under the sun (Ecclesiastes 1:9). Nothing happens in this world that is outside of His providence. God's perfect will deposes kings and raises up others as well. All of His prophetic word will be fulfilled. God is just as real today as He was yesterday. He is not an imaginary figure.

In order to change our problems on Earth, we must repent and turn to God by obeying His laws and commandments. We must go to the Father through Jesus Christ to change our hearts (John 14:6). Only the Heavenly Father can fix it, meeting our needs fully and forever by restoring peace in our minds and joy in our hearts. Fathers must continue to teach their children about God in order to help turn the hearts of the children back to the fathers and the hearts of the fathers back to the children.

References

Introduction

New King James Version, Bible Gateway, www.biblegateway.com

Farias, Bert M. "Turning the Hearts of Fathers to Their Children," September 9 18, 2014, www.charismanews.com/opinion/the-flaming-herald/45431-turning-the-hearts-of-fathers-to-their-children

Horst, Myron. "How to Turn the Hearts of Fathers to Their Children," (2015) www.biblicalresearchreports.com/turnheartsfathers.php

Wellman, Jack. "Better than I Deserve," "Turn the Hearts of the Fathers," June 2, 2013, blogs.christianpost.com/better-than-i-deserve/turn-the-hearts-of-the-fathers-16390/

Family Affair

New King James Version, Bible Gateway, www.biblegateway.com

Boehi, Dave. "The Cohabitation Complication," (2009) www.familylife.com/articles/topics/marriage/getting-married/choosing-a-spouse/the-cohabitation-complication

Carroll, Michael J. "Parenting-The Disengaged Parent" (2009) www.mijcar.com/parenting/disengagedparent.html

Joyce, Bryan. "Satan's Attack on the Family," May 2, 2010, www.truthandtidings.com/issues/2010/t20100502.php

Kruk, Edward. "Father Absence, Father Deficit, Father Hunger," Psychology Today, May 23, 2012, www.psychologytoday.com/blog/co-parenting-after-divorce/201205/father-absence-father-deficit-father-hunger

Moore, Sarah. "A Fatherless Generation," Relevant Magazine, July 7, 2008, www.relevantmagazine.com/life/whole-life/features/2721-a-fatherless-generation

Moskovitch, Deborah. "Estranged or Abandoned by a Parent: Are Children Scarred for Life?" The Huffington Post, June 20, 2011, http://www.huffingtonpost.com/deborah-moskovitch/oprahs-most-memorable-gue_1_b_869497.html

Peach, David. "How Does God Define Family, "What Christians Want to Know, http://www.whatchristianswanttoknow.com/how-does-god-define-family/#ixzz3w13hBbjD

Pritchard, Ray. "Portrait of a Dysfunctional Family" Keep Believing Ministries. September 6, 1992. http://www.keepbelieving.com/sermon/portrait-of-a-dysfunctional-family/

Lost Boys

New King James Version, Bible Gateway, www.biblegateway.com

Barnett, Brent. "Biblical Manhood-How the Bible Defines Masculinity,"www.relevantbibleteaching.com/site/cpage.asp?cpage_id=140025880&sec_id=140001239

Evans, Jimmy, Evans, Tammy. "Renegade Fathers, Renegade Children, "Marriage Today, December 8, 2010, www.marriagetoday.com/renegade-fathers-renegade-children/

Fox, Mark, "Prophet, Priest, Provider, Protector," June 10, 2009, http://familyintegratedchurch.com/index.php?option=com_content&view=article&id=25:prophet-priest-protector-provider&catid=2:articles&Itemid=30

Gadsen, O'Shan. "How Growing up Fatherlessness Can impact Current Relationships," The Good Men Project, October 6, 2013, www.goodmenproject.com/guyhood/how-growing-up-fatherless-can-impact-current-relationships/

Goins, Brian, "Do You Love Your Wife out of Obligation, "Family Life, 2011, http://www.familylife.com/articles/topics/marriage/staying-married/husbands/do-you-love-your-wife-out-of-obligation

Masters, Roy. "Cause of Homosexuality: Poor Parent-Child Relationships." Foundation of Human Understanding. (2010). https://www.fhu.com/articles/homosexual1.html

Mohler, Albert, "From Boy to Man—The Marks of Manhood," April 22, 2005 www.christianity.com/1325744/

Peterson, Jesse Lee, "Why Fathers Leave," June 16, 2007, World Net Daily, www.wnd.com/2007/06/42117/#kEEyrRQ6GtZZJWkE.99

Sanders, Ryan, 'The Father Absence Crisis in America," National Fatherhood Initiative, November 12, 2013,www.fatherhood.org/The-Father-Absence-Crisis-in-America

Schwarzwalder, Rob, "Boys Growing Up without Dads Remain Boys for Too Long, "Christian Post, August 11, 2014, http://www.christianpost.com/news/boys-growing-up-without-dads-remain-boys-for-too-long-124637/

Girls Gone Wild

New King James Version, Bible Gateway, www.biblegateway.com

Alvarez, Felicia, "4 Lies Culture Tells Us about Living Together before Marriage," Crosswalk, May 6, 2014, www.crosswalk.com/family/singles/4-lies-culture-tells-us-about-living-together-before-marriage.html

Barnett, Brent, "Biblical Womanhood-How the Bible Defines Femininity," www.relevantbibleteaching.com/site/cpage.asp?cpage_id=140011648&sec_id=140001239

Barras, Jonetta Rose, "Broken Families Lead to Broken Communities," Washington Post, April 8, 2015, www.washingtonpost.com/opinions/broken-families-lead-to-broken-communities/2015/04/08/041768c8-dca0-11e4-a500-1c5bb1d8ff6a_story.html?utm_term=.81a08b9c9236

Dean, Brooke, "Papa Pains: Signs You May Have Daddy Issues, "Madame Noire, www.madamenoire.com/187969/papa-pains-signs-you-may-have-daddy-issues/

Garrett-Akinsanya, BraVada, "Growing up Without a Father: The Impact on Girls and Women," Insight News, November 3, 2011, www.insightnews.com/2011/11/03/growing-up-without-a-father-the-impact-on-girls-and-women/

Hartwell-Walker, Marie, "Daughters Need Fathers, Too," Psych Central, May 17, 2016, www.psychcentral.com/lib/daughters-need-fathers-too/

Lewis, Patrice, "Fatherless Girls," World Net Daily, January 18, 2013, http://www.wnd.com/2013/01/fatherless-girls/

Makow, Henry, "Feminism Deprives Girls of Father's Love, "June 10, 2014, www.henrymakow.com/000998.html#sthash.j9cyjpV3.dpuf

McMenamin, Cindi, "Letting God Fill the Husband Void, "Crosswalk, October 20, 2010, www.crosswalk.com/faith/women/letting-god-fill-the-husband-void-11639816.html

Thorne, Saviela, "6 Personality Traits of the Proverbs 31 Woman, "The Praying Woman, (2015), http://theprayingwoman.com/2015/04/16/the-proverbs-31-woman/#comments

Media Influence

New King James Version, Bible Gateway, www.biblegateway.com

Akin, Stephanie, "Twitter Feed Glorifies Fights Featuring North Jersey Teens, Cops Say," The Record, July 6, 2015, http://www.northjersey.com/news/education/twitter-feed-glorifies-fights-featuring-north-jersey-teens-cops-say-1.1369273?page=all

Bindley, Katherine, "When Children Text All Day, What Happens to Their Social Skills?" Huffington Post, December 9, 2011, http://www.huffingtonpost.com/2011/12/09/children-texting-technology-social-skills_n_1137570.html

Coleman, Chrisena, "Do Teenage Girls Drive the Sexting Culture?" The Grio, April 8, 2011, www.thegrio.com/2011/04/08/are-teen-girls-driving-the-sexting-culture/

Hess, Patrick, "The Power Social Media has Over Teen Lives," Huffington Post, July 14, 2014, http://www.huffingtonpost.com/patrick-hess/the-power-social-media-has-over-teen-lives_b_5582497.html

Reese, Leilah, "Mixed Emotions about the Knockout Game," The Root, November 22, 2013, http://www.theroot.com/articles/culture/2013/11/my_mixed_feelings_about_the_knockout_game/

Petersen, Sarah, "Dumbing down Dad: How Media Present Husbands, Fathers as Useless," Desert News, February 27, 2013, http://www.deseretnews.com/article/865574236/Dumbing-down-Dad-How-media-present-husbands-fathers-as-useless.html

Waliszewski, Bob, "The Influence of Media," Focus on the Family, October 2007, http://www.focusonthefamily.com/parenting/kids-and-technology/combatting-cultural-influences/influence-of-media

Williams, Ray, "The decline of Fatherhood and the Male Identity Crisis," Psychology Today, June 19, 2011, www.psychologytoday.com/blog/wired-success/201106/the-decline-fatherhood-and-the-male-identity-crisis

Winnail, Douglas S., "How the Media Mold the World," Tomorrows World, January/February 2003, http://www.tomorrowsworld.org/magazines/2003/january-february/how-the-media-mold-the-world

Wygant, David, "Is Twitter and Facebook the End of Society?" Huffington Post, July 11, 2013, http://www.huffingtonpost.com/david-wygant/is-twitter-and-facebook-t_b_3574536.html

Impact the Community

New King James Version, Bible Gateway, www.biblegateway.com

Coulombe, Nikita, "The US is leading the Way in Fatherlessness and It's Hurting our Kids," The Elite Daily, June 18, 2015, http://elitedaily.com/life/culture/how-society-is-failing-fathers-photos/1069521/

Edelman, Peter,"Our History with Concentrated Poverty," Investing in What Works for America's Communities, http://www.whatworksforamerica.org/ideas/our-history-with-concentrated-poverty/#.V-26Y_krLct

Elder, Larry, "Gun Culture-What about the Fatherless Culture," World Net Daily, January 16, 2013, www.wnd.com/2013/01/gun-culture-what-about-the-fatherless-culture/

Forrest, Sharita, "Troubled Neighborhoods Deter Some Fathers from Child Involvement," Illinois News Bureau, October 25, 2012, https://news.illinois.edu/blog/view/6367/204954#

Franklin, Robert, "US Incarceration Rate Contributes to Fatherlessness," National Parents Organization, March 6, 2015, https://nationalparentsorganization.org/recent-articles?id=22225

Muehlenberg, Bill, "The Systematic War against Fathers," Culture Watch, February 28, 2014, www.billmuehlenberg.com/2014/02/28/the-systemic-war-against-fathers/

Pastor, James F., Toro, Nestor A., "Gangs in America-A Deadly Game," The Real Truth, November, 8, 2012, www.realtruth.org/articles/121106–001.html

Raspberry, William, "Poverty and the Father Factor, "Washington Post, August 1, 2005, http://www.washingtonpost.com/wp-dyn/content/article/2005/07/31/AR2005073101075.html?utm_term=.e1bffb20bc11

Do Ye Church

New King James Version, Bible Gateway, www.biblegateway.com

Coughlin, Paul, "Why Some Men Don't like Church, "Crosswalk, April 26, 2006, http://www.crosswalk.com/church/pastors-or-leadership/why-some-men-dont-like-church-1393422.html

Craven, Michael, "Fathers: Key to Their Children's Faith," Christian Post, June 19, 2011, http://www.christianpost.com/news/fathers-key-to-their-childrens-faith-51331/

Holmes, Phillip, "Finding the Fatherless: A Call to Fill the Gap," Desiring God, February 19, 2014, http://www.desiringgod.org/articles/finding-the-fatherless-a-call-to-fill-the-gap

Johnson, Christopher J.E. "501c3: The Devil's Church." Creation Liberty Evangelism. August 13, 2012. http://www.creationliberty.com/articles/501c3.php

Morris, Phillip, "Church Fails to Reach Black Men," The Plain Dealer, March 22, 2013, http://www.cleveland.com/metro/index.ssf/2009/03/church_fails_to_reach_black_me.html

Pivec, Holly, "The Feminization of the Church," Biola Magazine, spring 2006, www.magazine.biola.edu/article/06-spring/the-feminization-of-the-church/

Shaw, Joshua, "7 Actions to Engage the Men in your Church." March 12, 2012, http://pastors.com/7-actions-engage-men-church/

Vaughan, Harold, "Calling the Church Back to the Men." Christ Life Ministries, May 2006, www.christlifemin.org/home/blog/articles/calling-the-church-back-to-the-men/

Final Remarks

New King James Version, Bible Gateway, www.biblegateway.com

Barras, Jonetta Rose, "Broken Families Lead to Broken Communities," Washington Post, April 8, 2015, www.washingtonpost.com/opinions/broken-families-lead-to-broken-communities/2015/04/08/041768c8-dca0-11e4-a500-1c5bb1d8ff6a_story.html?utm_term=.81a08b9c9236

Beatty, Robert, "Let's Recommit to God, Redeem our Youth and Rebuild our Communities," South Florida Times, March 9, 2014, http://www.sfltimes.com/uncategorized/lets-recommit-to-god-redeem-our-youth-and-rebuild-our-communities

Coomer, Terry, "Cell Phones, Internet, and Social Media," Hope Biblical Counseling Center, July 22, 2015, http://hopebiblicalcounselingcenter.com/2015/07/865/

Daubenmire, Dave, "Where Have All the Fathers Gone, "News with Views, December 19, 2013, http://www.newswithviews.com/Daubenmire/dave350.htm

Sheriadan, Vern Poythress, "The Church as Family: Why Male Leadership in the Family Requires Male Leadership in the Church," Bible.org, Aril 14, 2005, https://bible.org/seriespage/13-church-family-why-male-leadership-family-requires-male-leadership-church

About the Author

Dwight is a freelance writer and poet of his first book *A Slice of Truth*. He has a passion to communicate God's design for the family. With that purpose in mind, Dwight seeks to give parents the tools and resources they need to be deepened spiritually, strengthen their marriages and relationships with their children, and encourage young people to make sound decisions to take their lives to the direction God has intended. Dwight has also presented multiple workshops and participated on discussion panels to a variety of audiences. He holds master's degrees from Chicago State and Governors State universities. He is also a member of Phi Beta Sigma Fraternity. Dwight has taught students on the high school and college levels for over fifteen years. He also serves as a deacon and Sunday school teacher at his church. Dwight enjoys spending time with his family, working out, watching college and professional sports, and listening to jazz and old school R&B music. Dwight DeRamus lives in the Chicagoland area, serving as a husband for over twenty years and being a proud father of two sons. Log in online at www.disappearingdads.com

www.ingramcontent.com/pod-product-compliance
Lightning Source LLC
Chambersburg PA
CBHW050439010526
44118CB00013B/1592